WHAT IS YOUR

LIFE?

HOW TO MAKE REAL FRIENDS, GROW YOUR FAITH AND CHANGE THE WORLD

BRETT LONGO

Luhado Publishing

Published by Luhado Publishing

Cover Design by Brett Longo

Proofread by Denise Harmer, DHarmerEdits@gmail.com, http://deniseharmer.weebly.com/

LIBRARY OF CONGRESS CATALOGING-IN-PUBLICATION DATA

Longo, Brett, 1964-

What is Your Life? How to make real friends, grow your faith and change the world/Brett Longo.

p. cm.

ISBN 978-0-9987746-8-8 (Paperback)

1. Youth-Religious Life.   2. Christian Life.   3. Mentoring – Religious Life   4. Spiritual Warfare

To my Lord Jesus.

Here is the book You called me to write.

May You use it to advance Your Kingdom.

To my children, Hannah, Luke and Dominic.

Thank you for allowing me to write this when you wanted to play.

To my wife, Tanya.

Thank you for understanding the call.

TABLE OF CONTENTS

I can do all things

through Christ who

strengthens me.

Philippians 4:13

The value of life is not computed by its duration but by its donation.

Philosopher William James

You are a necessary part of a greater Plan!

Author Unknown

Jesus sent his twelve harvest hands out with this charge:

Don't begin by traveling to some far-off place to convert unbelievers. And don't try to be dramatic by tackling some public enemy. Go to the lost, confused people right here in the neighborhood. Tell them that the kingdom is here. Bring health to the sick. Raise the dead. Touch the untouchables. Kick out the demons. You have been treated generously, so live generously.

Matthew 10:5-8 (MSG)

INTRODUCTION

The other day I happened to see a news clip on TV. Six soldiers from Egypt had been killed trying to defend their embassy in Iran. However heroic this may have been, it seemed so insignificant. To think that six young soldiers lost their lives for what the world will forget in just a few days was devastating. I started to think, *Can life really be explained?* As soldiers, they were probably young, possibly married and with children. It is frustrating to believe that their lives were taken short for political reasons. Then I started to think about all the generations of the past whose lives were shortened for political reasons. It transcends time. Each war, each conflict—men, women, children all leaving this earth prematurely.

Life is not permanent. We see life come and go all the time. I began to wonder, *If life isn't permanent, then what is?* Then it hit me! Nations, cultures, traditions, ideologies, principalities, and powers—they are what is permanent on this earth. Men die for their country in war so that their country will live. The sanctity of human life is lost for the betterment of a mass of land defined by its borders, its ideologies, its traditions, its powers. Simply stated, it is the *cause* of such things that lives on, not the people. Apparently, we are wired to live for a cause, to live for something that will continue to exist well after our years on this earth. It is almost as if the cause is why we are here whether we subscribe to it or not.

In a unique way, I wrote *What Is Your Life?* to inspire you to live for the cause of Christ. I took a hard look at what it means to be a Christian teen in your world today, and how you can interact with those who may not share your views. First you must be the Christian Jesus calls you to be before you can do what He calls you to do. Therefore, I divided *What Is Your Life?* into two parts:

Part One, "Being," starts with understanding how Satan has legitimate concerns about your generation. He feels threatened by your generation, as he should, because your generation, it appears, is destined for greatness. Next, you will learn of the divine secrets of God and how these secrets can be used to love even the unlovable. Then you will learn how to go deep into relationships and the need for prayer if you are going to make a difference in the world.

Part two, "Doing," begins with understanding how a cause gains momentum in this world. It then delves into why God has chosen your generation to lead the biggest revival the world has ever seen. Finally, the book ends with a challenge. Living for a cause greater than yourself requires courage and integrity. This challenge may be the hardest you've ever taken.

I designed this book to be read a chapter a week during the summer. It requires that you ask a mentor, someone who is strong in his or her faith, of the same gender, and at least ten years older than you, to read this book with you. When your mentor accepts this assignment, he or she will have access to another book, *The Mentor's Manual*. This manual has challenges in them. Each week you are to read the chapter, then get one-on-one with your mentor to help you digest what you've read. Your mentor will be challenging you to reach out to others as you learn the God principles in this book. Some weeks, you'll be asked by your mentor to complete a challenge. Along with your mentor, you are to complete your challenge. If you are part of a youth group which has accepted this challenge, then you'll be doing your challenge with others as a group.

Each challenge gets progressively harder, so another ground rule you must follow is that you can't continue to the next challenge until you've completed the last. I like to think of one's faith as a muscle; if you exercise it, it will get stronger. Each challenge requires a greater measure of faith than the challenge before, so it wouldn't make sense to keep on going if you don't think you can complete a prior challenge. Once you've completed the challenge (ideally right after), sit down with your mentor to talk about the challenge with him or her. He or she will have some questions to ask to open a dialog with you. This should be in an environment where you can share your feelings, so if Starbucks is too public and you are concerned someone may overhear your conversation, then try to find a more private setting. Regardless, when you share, be open and honest with your feelings and the experience in general.

"Why so many rules?" you ask. I designed this book to inspire teens in the church to get out and serve their community. If done in the way it has been laid out, you will have expressed your faith in a way that all your friends can accept. According to Thom and Jess Rainer in their book *The Millennials*, 85% of teens don't want to have anything to do with religion (i.e., going to church). To them, religion is nothing more than a bunch of embittered hypocrites who manipulate their religion to serve themselves and no other. We are going to shatter that view by getting out there and serving others.

There is no greater way to live than to live for a cause greater than yourself. *What Is Your Life?* will require courage and integrity, as you make a stand for Christ in your community. If you are ready to be part of such a cause, begin looking for your mentor, invite him or her to come along side of you, and read on!

Brett Longo

April 2018, Valley Center, CA

PART ONE — BEING

Do not conform any longer to the pattern of this world ...

Romans 12:2 NIV

If you belonged to the world, it would love you as its own. As it is, you do not belong to the world, but I have chosen you out of the world.

John 15:19 NIV

1

SATAN NEEDS YOU

Then the king ordered Ashpenaz, the chief of his officials, to bring in some of the sons of Israel, including some of the royal family and of the nobles, youths in whom was no defect, who were good-looking, showing intelligence in every branch of wisdom, endowed with understanding and discerning knowledge, one who had ability for serving the king's court; and he ordered him to teach them the literature and language of the Chaldeans. The king appointed for them a daily ration from the king's choice food and from the wine which he drank, and appointed that they should be educated three years, at the end of which they were to enter the king's personal service.

Daniel 1:3-5

Give me the children, I will give you a nation. When an opponent declares "I will not come over to your side," I calmly say, "Your child belongs to us already. What are you? You will pass on. Your descendants, however, now stand in the new camp. In a short while they will know nothing else but this new community."

Adolph Hitler (1939)

As crazy as this statement from Adolf Hitler is, it is true. Hitler knew if he could change the open-minded children, he could indoctrinate them to believe in his twisted way of thinking. Unfortunately, Hitler wasn't the first to come up with this idea. This strategy has played out throughout time: influence the minds of the children, and over time, you can get what you want.

In the book of Daniel, the Bible speaks of another man, a man who, much like Adolf Hitler, wanted to establish a one-world government and a one-world religion. His name was Nebuchadnezzar (pronounced *Neb a Kenezer*), king of Babylon; and his empire had progressed to the far ends of the earth. The only land he had yet to conquer was a small country the size of New Jersey where the one and only true God was worshiped. He knew little of this God, yet understood the devotion of this God's people, the Israelites. And because of this devotion, Nebuchadnezzar knew these people would never devote themselves to him.

Understanding this, Nebuchadnezzar countered with an ingenious plan. He decided to take these God-worshiping people out of their land and force them to live in his. Worse yet, he even went as far as to take seventy of Israel's finest youth: young men your age, of Israelite nobility, the leaders of Israel's tomorrow, making them live with him in his palace. If he could get these boys away from their cultural beliefs and religious doctrines, he could train them to live in a culture where another god was worshiped, the big Neb, King Nebuchadnezzar himself. Then as men, with children of their own, he could send them back to the land from which they were taken and replace their traditional religious beliefs with his. Over the course of just three generations' time, or roughly sixty years, this culture would be transformed to believe in one king, with one-world government and one-world religion.

There is something to be said for having faith like a child, as Jesus described in Matthew 18:2. It embodies a trust that stems from innocence. To a new believer, this innocent faith can be challenged and often is. How many friends do you have who gave their life to Jesus in grade school but now wonder if He really is "The Way"? It is much easier to persuade a youthful Christian to defy God than an older one. The saying, "You can't teach an old dog a new trick" isn't too far from the truth. Nebuchadnezzar knew this in 600 BC, Hitler knew this in 1939, and Satan has known this forever.

The Bible describes Satan as the "Ruler of this World," and the "Father of Lies" (John 14:30; John 8:44). He has misled all but those who claim to be followers of Jesus Christ. He, like Nebuchadnezzar, has a desire to see all bow to him. His thorn, America, is much like the thorn of Israel to Nebuchadnezzar, and the tactic Nebuchadnezzar used in 600 BC is the same tactic Satan uses on our land today—**go after you, the young leaders of tomorrow.**

As the Bible states, he is quite crafty: a serpent who has slithered on this earth for much longer than you or I (Revelation 12:9; Genesis 3:1). His desire is to turn our hearts away from the one true God and fall in love with the idols of feeling good, looking good, being right, and being comfortable. These are the subtle yet pervasive idols of our time, and they reflect the truth of our hearts. Worse yet, they are found in the hearts of Christian believers as much as those who don't believe. They come from the choice to serve the flesh rather than God. This has been Satan's objective from the beginning. Weren't Adam and Eve eating the fruit because Satan convinced them they could be like God? Although his strategies have changed, Satan's objective remains the same: to turn man away from God, his heavenly Father. What better way to hurt God than to go after his precious children? He and his low-life thugs that we call demons desire to see you and the rest of the world worship Satan, and the best way to make someone worship Satan is to pull his attention away from the Father and onto the selfish indulgences of feeling good, looking good, being right, and being comfortable.

Satan's Attack on Your Land

The attack began in the 1960s. Like Nebuchadnezzar, Satan looked to replace the dominant Judeo-Christian culture with a culture where one could worship whomever and whatever he wanted. The great freedom movement of the 60s was a time in America when the youth decided they wanted to express themselves however they chose. His simple message was being broadcast on the radio, on the newly invented television, and even in the lecture halls and auditoriums of universities throughout this great nation. College professors, many of whom claimed to be the voice of socialism, spoke lies into the pure naïve minds of America. "What was the message?" you ask. The same one he offered Adam and Eve some 6,000 years ago: "You can be free if you eat of this fruit." We are all like sheep easily led astray (Isaiah 53:6).

To create immorality is to create lack of respect for human life, and to create lack of respect for human life is to create hopelessness. And to be without hope is to be without understanding of God and the message of hope that lies within Jesus Christ. Remember, the desire of

Satan is to change the face of this nation, and he, like Nebuchadnezzar, is out to do it within three generations' time. If the 60s movement was the beginning of immorality in our land, then the children of those influenced by the 1960s movements would be the **first generation** under Satan's influence. These were the children born in the late 1950s and early 1960s when recreational drugs, divorce, single parenting, and abortion became as American as McDonald's, Coca-Cola, and Chevrolet.

Their children, the **second generation** under Satan's attack, would have been born in the late 1970s and early 1980s. They are the children who've survived the war on the womb where one out of every three were murdered. Likewise, they were the first to experience the breakdown of nuclear family and the perversion of MTV, Jerry Springer, and pornography as a normal way of life.

Their children, the **third generation** under Satan's attack, would in turn be born in the 1990s to early 2000s. They will be the grandchildren of those from the freedom movement of the 1960s. Will they know right from wrong? Will they understand God and the hope that rests in Jesus Christ? Will they understand the Christian heritage this country was founded on? These answers depend largely upon you.

With the guidance of God's word, your mentor and Holy Spirit, you have the power to fight against the moral decay Satan has put into motion upon our land. It is by no coincidence you are reading this book right now. God will use you mightily if you choose. The question is, "Are you willing?" Do you have a desire in your heart to stand for the God you believe in? Or is it more important for you to look good, feel good, be right, and be comfortable? Only time will tell.

Four Worlds Operating Simultaneously in One

The world you live in can be divided into four distinct arenas or realms. What makes your family, your school, your community, county, state, country, and culture different from any other is how these realms are embraced, accepted/rejected by you and those you live with. All four realms are real, whether you acknowledge their existence or not.

The physical realm is experienced through your body. It is the part of the world you see, taste, touch, smell, and hear, i.e., experience through your senses. All materialism exists in this realm (including things like your car, your PlayStation or XBox, your iPod, clothes, and jewelry). Money is what drives this world. In fact, money is nothing more than printed paper that allows one to own physical realm "stuff," and nothing more. Have you ever wondered why Westernized culture places so much importance on the physical realm?

The intellectual realm is experienced through your mind. It is made up of what you know, the way you reason, and what you believe. Information drives this realm. In fact, the ability to store, assimilate, and reason allows one to enter into this realm. Studying subjects in school, understanding good from bad, reading, philosophizing, and comprehending God all require one to exist in this realm.

The emotional realm is experienced through your heart. It is made up of feelings. In fact, the emotional realm is what you feel. Internal thoughts drive this realm. These thoughts trigger fear, anger, frustration, joy, contentment, and fatigue. The way you perceive situations in your life (i.e., your attitude) drives this world.

And finally, there is the spiritual realm. It exists independent of you. All the other realms you experience are within your body. The spiritual realm is different. It is like another world in another dimension co-existing within the physical world. At any time, however, this realm can enter your mind, body, and soul, with or without your consent. Sound freaky? Hold on; it gets even more intriguing. **This realm and its powers drive the other three realms you live in.**

There are two forces at work in this realm. One stands for goodness, honesty, and purity, while the other stands for evil, deception, and destruction. Your choices affect how these spiritual forces influence your life. If you so choose to follow the force of goodness, honesty, and purity, then the Holy Spirit will dwell within you and protect you from the forces of evil, deception, and destruction. On the other hand, if you choose to follow the force of evil, deception, and destruction, you are prone to having an evil spirit dwell within you. By your choices, you either become an ally or an enemy to the King of Kings, Jesus Christ. "But what if I don't choose either side?" you ask. By abstaining from choosing, you default to the side of evil and allow Satan and his demons to influence you to fight against Jesus Christ (Luke 9:50).

Another way of looking at this realm is to see it as a matrix. This matrix has been carefully orchestrated by Satan so that you don't even see the influence it has on your life. According to the Bible, you were created for a reason (Ephesians 2:10). It isn't by chance you came into being as the public schools teach. No, your purpose has been strategically planned by God. He has you exactly where you need to be at exactly the right time. His call on your life is just as important as the heroes we read of in the Bible (Jeramiah 29:11). To believe that God created you without reason, is to fall directly into Satan's trap of living a life without purpose and meaning. Interestingly, a movie called *The Matrix* perfectly illustrates how Satan and his demons have done this.

The Matrix

For our struggle is not against flesh and blood, but against... [*The Matrix.*]

Ephesians 6:12

Have you ever had a dream Neo, that you were so sure it was real? What if you were unable to wake from that dream? How would you know the difference between the dream world and the real world?

The Matrix, 1999; Warner Brothers

As for you, you were dead in your transgressions and sins, in which you used to live when you followed the ways of this world and of the ruler of the kingdom of the air, the spirit who is now at work in those who are disobedient. All of us lived among them at one time, gratifying the cravings of our sinful nature and following its desires and thoughts. Like the rest, we were by nature objects of wrath.

Ephesians 2:1-3 NIV

In 1999, Warner Brothers released a sci-fi action thriller called *The Matrix*. With special effects never seen before, its blend of intense fight scenes and a multilayered story line, *The Matrix*, winner of four Oscars, grossed 460 million dollars and became the first film to sell over one million DVDs. Its subtle yet pervasive story line proved to be eerily symbolic of the illusion the forces of evil play on our naive lives.

In the movie, a man resembling a secret service agent stands looking out of a sky rise window upon the busy streets below. He is known as a "Centium Program," and he is paradoxically analogous to the demons that influence our world today. Speaking about the matrix (i.e., the world), he says, "Have you ever stood and stared at it? It's beauty. It's genius. Billions of people just living out their lives, oblivious."

The Matrix is a powerful metaphor of God's desire to seek us out of a sinful fallen world so that we may, in turn, serve Him to seek out another. This metaphor illustrates the polarizing war being played out in each of our hearts.

The movie starts out by introducing a young man named Thomas Anderson who has found life to be a grind, getting up every day to go to work to pay bills. It is without meaning or reason and has no vision. He is living a double life working by day for a software company, then pirating this company's software on the underground market by night. He is tired, tired of living in a world where the harder he works, the more meaningless his life becomes. This worldly fatigue drives him to search for deep meaningful answers. Why am I here, and what is life all about? His search takes him to the matrix, a mystic and unusual computer program that seems to have the answers he is looking for.

The matrix, which speaks to him through his computer, gives him a new name, Neo, and begins to open his mind to a deeper reality. Through a series of events, the matrix directs young Neo to an underground bar where he sees a beautiful young woman approaching him.

"Hello Neo," the woman says in a low, seductive tone.

Looking somewhat perplexed Neo asks, "How do you know my name?"

"I know a lot about you."

"Who are you?"

"My name is Trinity," she responds.

"The Trinity, that cracked the IRS D-Base?" he asks in amazement.

"That was a long time ago."

"Jesus!"

Somewhat bewildered by his response, Trinity asks, "What?"

"I just thought, um, you were a guy."

"Most guys do."

"That was on your computer! How did you do that?"

With a sense of urgency in her voice, she continues, "Right now all I can tell you is that you are in danger. I brought you here to warn you."

"What?"

Trinity walks closer. Now speaking softly into his ear, "They are watching you, Neo."

"Who is?"

"Please, just listen. I know why you're here, Neo. I know what you've been doing. I know why you hardly sleep, why you live alone, and why night after night you sit at your computer. You're looking for Him. I know because I was once looking for the same thing. And when He found me, He told me I wasn't really looking for Him; I was looking for an answer. It is the question that drives us, Neo. The question that brought you here. You know the question, just as I did."

Staring blankly into the floor, Neo manages to slowly exhale. "What is the matrix?"

Seeing that he is following her line of logic, she continues, "The Answer is up there Neo, and It's looking for you. And It will find you if you want It to."

The Matrix, 1999; Warner Bros.

http://bit.ly/Neo_meets_Trinity

This scene metaphorically illustrates the beginning of a Christian's walk, a stirring of questions within, a gnawing hunger for answers to "Who am I, where am I going after I die, what is life all about, and why am I here?" However simple these questions may be, we find them hard to wrap our minds around and come up with an answer. Could there really be one Answer? Isn't the Answer different for us all? Wrestling with such questions isn't easy. It takes some deep introspective thought that seems kind of scary. What if I can't figure out why I'm here and what my life is all about? What if I'm here to run an orphanage in Mexico when all I can think about is dancing on Broadway or playing in the NFL? Can I really answer the question "Who am I?" After all, for as many people as walk the earth, aren't there that many reasons? So, we stop asking the questions. It is easier to busy ourselves with school projects, clubs, academics, sports, cheerleading, dance, music, theater, art, or gaming—anything to cover up that which gnaws on our conscience.

Then, the brevity of life rears its ugly head. A close friend, grandfather, great-grandmother, or great athlete in his prime suddenly dies; a cousin or nephew is born. The questions come back. Why do we have to die? Where did I come from? Why am I here? And... where am I going after this? It is at this point the soils of the heart are ready for God's truth to take root and grow (Matthew 13:18-23). A friend or loved one, someone who seems to care, shows up, someone who has the Answer to all these questions. It is the Answer that is looking for them, and It will find them when they are ready (Revelation 3:20).

The movie continues with young Neo beginning to see the Answer. He is called by a man named Morpheus whom he has connected with online. Morpheus has caught Neo's attention. He sees Neo's longing for something better, and he has the Answer. With comments such as, "I don't know if you're ready for what I want to show you, but unfortunately you and I have run out of time. They are coming for you,

Neo, and I don't know what they are going to do," and "You are the one, Neo. You see, you may have spent the last two years looking for me, but I've spent my entire life looking for you," Morpheus is able to lure Neo into meeting with him. They agree to meet in an old, unmarked, abandoned building on the outskirts of the city. The room is dark and cold. Two wingback chairs face one another, Neo dressed simply in jeans and a T-shirt sitting in one, and Morpheus, wearing a long, leather trench coat and sunglasses in the other. Leaning forward in his chair, Morpheus extends his hands. In each palm rests a pill, one red, the other blue.

Looking intently into Neo's eyes, Morpheus says, "If you take the blue pill, the story ends; you wake up in your bed and believe what you want to believe. Take the red pill, you stay in wonderland, and I show you how deep the rabbit hole goes. Remember, all I'm offering is the **Truth**, nothing more."

The Matrix, 1999; Warner Bros.
http://bit.ly/blue_or_red_pill

The Answer now lies before him, yet he must choose, like us all, to accept the deep meaning of his life. This is no different from the day you chose to accept **Jesus** into your heart. The Bible reads, "and you will know the Truth, and the Truth will make you free." (John 8:32). The Hebrew term for "truth" means reality. Then you will know the Reality, and the Reality will make you free. You had to choose. Do I take the blue pill and die to an unconscious denial, or do I take the red pill and wake up to the Reality that I have been born into, bondage (sin), and can only be saved by grace? It is appointed for men to die once and after this comes judgment (Hebrews 9:27). It is this judgment we are talking about. Do you want to see wonderland? Do you want to know how deep the rabbit hole goes?

Neo has received the fate of the red pill. He is born again. Reality now stands before him. Reclined in a chair and attached to a computerized machine on a small spaceship called the Nebuchadnezzar (there's that name again), Neo is about to enter the Matrix (World) with his mentor Morpheus at his side.

Morpheus says, "Your appearance now is what we call residual self-image. It is the mental projection of your digital self."

Running his hands along a winged back chair, Neo asks, "This, this isn't real?"

"What is real? How do you define real? If you are talking about what you can feel, what you can smell, what you can taste and see, then real is simply electrical signals interpreted by your brain. This is the world that you know. The world as it was at the end of the 20th century. It exists now only as a part of a neural interactive simulation that we call the Matrix. You've been living in a dream world, Neo. This is the world as it exists today. Welcome to the desert of the real... Fate, it seems, is not without a sense of irony." Morpheus continues, "What is the Matrix? Control. The Matrix is a computer-generated dream world, built to keep us under control in order to change a human being into this. [*Morpheus holds up a battery*]"

"No, I don't believe it. It's not possible."

"I didn't say it would be easy, Neo, I just said it would be the Truth."

Neo, now starting to panic at the reality he is facing, cries out, "Stop! Let me out! Let me out! I want out!"

The Matrix, 1999; Warner Bros.
http://bit.ly/Morpheus_explains_what_is_real

This scene isn't too far from the truth. We all carry a sub or unconscious mind. It works to store data like a computer. Every moment of every experience is logged onto neural pathways that make up the hard drive of our brains. These pathways can be triggered by familiar smells, tastes, or sounds—anything that has input into the brain from the sixth month of pregnancy until we die. Once triggered, these senses rise to our conscience in the form of memory. From this data bank, we start to put together perceptions or beliefs of what is right and good, and what is wrong and bad. It has often been said our perceptions become our reality. Although we are unaware of our subconscious interaction, when making choices, we are checking in with our belief system or perception of reality all the time. Now, if Satan can alter your belief system at the subconscious level, he can persuade you to make wrong or bad choices without you consciously knowing it. Hmm? Does that sound just a little like Satan?

Lies, Lies and More Lies

It has been said, "If you tell a lie often and long enough, people will start to believe it." You are living in a world full of lies. Our world, the Matrix we live in, is controlled by Satan (Ephesians 2:2; John 14:30). He is the father of lies (John 8:44). From the moment we enter into this world until the time we die, we are being exposed to lies.

Young women, the fashion magazines, and media scream at you, "You're not pretty enough. You weigh too much. You're not tall enough. You'll never have a man." Guys, the competitive world keeps knocking on your door, "You aren't good enough. You don't have what it takes to compete, you are going to lose." We keep striving to look a certain way and have certain things, because the prince of this world has built into the system a lie that says this is the way to happiness, contentment, and love.

Without them you are a "nobody, a big fat loser." The lies continue to pound on us over and over again. The neural pathways harden, and we begin to believe what we are hearing. We become captives, cowering from the very blessings God has for us in our life, and it is all because of what we believe. Soon we settle, disqualify, and discount ourselves from having what God wants for our very lives.

This reality may overwhelm you much as it did Neo. You may not believe it! I didn't say it would be easy; I just said it would be the truth. The question that now we must ask is, "Then how do we know truth?" If truth comes from our perception, and our perception is of a world full of lies, then how can I know truth? Pontius Pilate once asked the same question (John 18:38). Young Neo found himself processing the same question. Hours after his encounter with reality, he was approached by Morpheus.

"I can't go back, can I?" a dejected Neo asked.

"No, but if you could, would you really want to? The mind has trouble letting go." Seeing the hopelessness and despair in Neo, Morpheus continued, "When the Matrix [world] was first built, there was a man [Jesus] born inside who had the ability to change what He wanted, to remake the Matrix [world] as He saw fit. It was He who freed the first of us, taught us the Truth. As long as the Matrix exists, the human race will never be free. After He died, the Oracle prophesied His return; that His coming would hail the destruction of the Matrix, end the war, and bring freedom to the people."

The Matrix, 1999; Warner Bros.
http://bit.ly/I_cant_go_back

The Bible says Jesus is Truth (John 14:6). The Bible also says His word is Truth (Psalm 119:160; John 1:14; John 17:17). The Bible, God's word, is our anchor. It holds us to His law and, in fact, is what our nations laws come from (see Notables below). When we don't know His word, we are in danger of being misled (Psalm 119:118; Isaiah 9:15-16, 47:10; Colossians 2:2-4). This is why so many men have devoted their entire lives to the study of the Bible. A collection of Sixty-Six books written over three thousand years by forty different authors on three different continents and yet its principles never contradict themselves. Inspired by God (2 Timothy 3:16-17), its truth runs deep enough to divide soul from spirit, joints, and marrow, and judge the thoughts and attitudes of the heart (Hebrews 4:12).

Morpheus has made a difference in Neo's life. Not only has he saved Neo from death and destruction, but he has also introduced him to a life of vision and purpose. To be a mentor or coach is nothing short of a huge undertaking. It is an investment in time and energy. It requires selling the one you are mentoring to capture a vision so great only God can fulfill. It requires continual encouragement to reach for greater possibility. It also requires discipline and calling one out of the comfort he or she lives in. It is to believe that the one you are mentoring will one day rise higher than yourself.

The greatest mentor who ever walked on this earth was Jesus Christ. He devoted all of Himself to what the rest of the world had labeled a bunch of losers: Mathew the thief, embezzler, tax collector; Peter and Andrew, uneducated fishermen; John, some punk teenager. They were being led by a man who talked to prostitutes and touched lepers; who slept on the ground, rarely getting the opportunity to bathe. And He says of those who will follow Him, "I tell you the truth, whomever believes in me will do the same things that I do. Those who believe will do even greater things than these ..." (John 14:12 NCV).

The Losers

One thing God loves to do is get his hands on those everyone else has written off. It is the losers, the nobodies, the ones no one sees potential in that He uses so mightily. Think about it. Who gets the credit if some nobody suddenly becomes a "somebody" in the world? Abraham, Moses, Joshua, Gideon, Daniel, Shadrach, Meshach, and Abed-nego, David before Goliath, plus many more were written off by society much like the disciples, and all were used mightily by God.

In *The Matrix*, Morpheus sees young Neo in much the same light. His answer to Neo has given him a new Hope to continue. Now Morpheus must guide young Neo's mind toward the truth. He does this by revealing the belief system of lies young Neo has been believing (2 Corinthians 5:17; Hebrews 8:13). Morpheus encourages young Neo while instructing him during one of his training sessions.

"The Matrix is a system, Neo. That system is our enemy. When you're inside, what do you see? Businessmen, teachers, lawyers, carpenters—the very minds of the people we are trying to save. But until we do, these people are still a part of that system, and that makes them our enemy. You have to understand, most of these people are not ready to be unplugged. And many of them are so inert, so hopelessly dependent upon the system that they will fight to protect it. Are you listening to me Neo?"

The Matrix, 1999; Warner Bros.
http://bit.ly/The_Matrix_is_a_System

Being sold to the lie that one must achieve within the system to succeed requires many years of subconscious programming. Deprogramming this belief system may require much time and effort. For many coming to know and understand Jesus for the first time, this is the biggest obstacle of all. They simply cannot fathom being loved for who they are, because they have lived in a belief system that has dictated otherwise. Often, they believe they must "clean themselves up" before God can accept them. This is a lie driven by the fear of failure. Even those who've supposedly given their life to Christ remain stuck in a performance trap, believing that they must work to gain God's approval. Statistics show that as we grow older our belief systems or perceptions become harder and harder to break. With minds that are open and flexible, 64% of all believers come to know Jesus Christ before they reach the age of eighteen (data from Barna Research Group, *Evangelism is Most Effective Among Kids*, October 11, 2004). This means you don't have much time to reach your friends who are lost.

Neo's discipleship continues. He is slowly starting to see the vision. He is slowly becoming aware of the calling on his life. Every time he takes a step in faith, he builds confidence in truth, and sees more of the vision of who he is for others. Yet, he is still not ready to save the world. More training is required.

"This. This isn't the Matrix?" asks Neo.

"No. It's another training program to teach you one thing. If you are not one of us, you are one of them," responds Morpheus.

Looking at what appears to be a man wearing a dark suit and sunglasses, Neo asks, "What are they?"

"Centium Programs," replies Morpheus. "They can move in and out of any software still hard wired to their system. That means that anyone we haven't unplugged is potentially an agent. Inside the matrix, they are everyone, and they are no one. We have survived by hiding from them and running from them. They are the gate keepers. They are guarding all the doors. They are holding all the keys, which means sooner or later someone is going to have to fight them. Their strength and speed is built in a world based on rules. Because of that they will never be as strong or as fast as you can be."

"What are you trying to tell me, that I can dodge bullets?"

"No, Neo, I'm trying to tell you that when you are ready, you won't have to."

The Matrix, 1999; Warner Bros.

http://bit.ly/Centium_Programs

The Spiritual Forces of Evil

To the Christian, "Centium Programs" are analogous to spiritual forces of evil in the heavenly realms (Ephesians 6:12), demons and demonic influences that carry strongholds within our minds, over our schools, cities, and land. They can torment Christians and dwell within non-Christians. They desensitize our conscience through the subtle programming of the subconscious. It is important to remember here that these demonic influences are the devil and his fallen angels (Isaiah 14:12). They do not carry the ability to be everywhere all the time. Therefore, they must start small fires (lies) here and there. Over the course of time, however, these lies become raging and out of control. To them, deceiving a mind results in deceiving a family which results in deceiving a community. They then inhabit this community, turning it into a stronghold of deception.

To give you an example of this, let's look at the decision of Roe vs. Wade in 1973, when abortion became legal in our land. To many, it appeared as a small victory; after all, only 14 women in 1,000 of reproductive age were having an abortion. By 1979, however, that total grew to 24 women in 1,000. Abortion totals by 1979 had reached 1.5

million babies annually (see Notables at the end of this chapter for reference).

By desensitizing the moral conscience of people through this Supreme Court decision, Satan and his demons have been able to influence the murder of over 50 million babies in the womb, and Americans seem to be OK with it. Remember, this is what Satan and his followers desire—to create lack of respect for human life and the hopelessness that follows. It is a matter of time before he and his followers are cast into the lake of burning sulfur forever (Revelation 20:10). His desire is to bring as many of God's precious creation with him as he can.

The Matrix is an awesome illustration of the Christian mission. A young man is being called by a mystic and unusual system. He is not sure if he can trust these people, but his inner nature is "longing" for something different from what he has. His search ends with the Answer he has always been looking for. Every step he takes is built upon the last, and each step requires a greater measure of faith; yet each step brings him closer to the Truth. There is a battle for his life. Two entities warring over his being: Satan wanting to deceive with lies, and God wanting to reveal with truth.

In the end stands a man or woman who has been exposed to the Truth, and the Truth has set him or her free (John 8:32). Young Neo was chosen, much like you, to enter into the world and expose the lie, to battle against the very enemy who sucks the life from us all. In the end, by choice, Neo **believes** the powers that lie within him are far greater than those possessed by the enemy (1 John 4:4). They no longer have a stronghold on his mind. He is free indeed, and the compassion to free the world burns within him.

You are no different from Neo. You are the one—chosen by God and bought for a price (Ephesians 1:11; 1 Corinthians 7:23; Romans

8:29-33). At one time you sat in a cocoon, unaware of the tentacles of Satan's world sucking the life blood out of you, but you made a choice to take the red pill and be born again through Jesus Christ. Free your mind. Believe that the strongholds of doubt, fear, worry, and disbelieving have no dominion over you (Matthew 21:21; Ephesians 6:12). God has chosen you to step into the world and war against the rulers, authorities, and powers of this dark world, and against the spiritual forces of evil.

What is required of you is to understand Satan's attack on your land and the weapons God has given you to fight against those attacks. This is where the action and super drama of *The Matrix* differs from the reality of the Bible. Your weapons are not of destruction like those in the movie, but the weapons of love as described in the Bible (Ephesians 6:10-18). We do not war against evil with evil; we war against evil the way Jesus did, with courage, compassion, gentleness, love, God's word, and prayer. By using the wisdom of truth, and a willingness to die to self for the sake of others (Romans 12:1-2) you can overcome Satan's attack on your land.

Neo had to spend time in training to war against his enemy. So, too, do you. The beginnings of this book are established to prepare you for the Matrix (i.e., world) that lies just outside your bedroom door. Going into the Matrix without the weapons of your warfare is grounds for suicide. Satan and his "Centium Programs" will surely overcome you.

Finally, you have a special agent who protects you in the spiritual realm. His name is Holy Spirit and He can do many things (Isaiah 11:1-7), one of which is to protect you from death. Satan cannot kill you, but he can make your life a living Hell. My encouragement to you: do not enter into the matrix until you are ready to do so.

Just as Neo depended on Morpheus, you too will need a mentor, someone to help you keep a right perspective on your way of being in your friends' lives, someone who's willing to encourage, stand with and for you, spend time with you, create vision in your heart, listen, and believe you are the one. He or she will show you the door, but it is up to you to walk through it (Revelation 3:8).

If you haven't done so already, it is time to find your Morpheus, someone who is at least ten years older than you, is a wise Christian, and is of the same gender. Look for someone in your church or family whom you greatly respect for their love of Jesus and invite him or her to be a part of your journey. Once you've invited someone to be your mentor, encourage that person to read this book along with you. Have them log into www.theg2c.org/mentor to receive a copy of the *Mentor's Manual* that goes along with this book. Once your mentor has accepted your invite, let your Youth Pastor know who your mentor is. If you don't have a youth group that you attend, no worries, you can still do this with your mentor.

Each week you'll be asked to read a chapter of this book. Some weeks you will be asked to take on a challenge with your mentor. You will need to meet with your mentor to receive the challenge. Each challenge gets progressively harder, so you won't be able to take on a new challenge until you've completed the prior challenge.

When you are ready, get with your mentor. He or she may have a challenge for you so be ready. May the Force (Holy Spirit) be with you.

QUOTABLES:

"So much of our life is in pursuit of one thing—Please, somebody just love me. Someone care about me just the way I am. We dress a certain way, wear our hair a certain way. We pierce our bodies and buy clothes we don't need, buy cars and stereos we don't need. We work out for endless hours in the gym. Why? Please, somebody, look twice. The lie becomes so much the norm that we tend to judge those who aren't striving like us. We chastise them as fat, ugly, poor, gross, geeks, nobodies... We alienate them with our un-favored looks, all the while not understanding the lies we have succumbed to in our very minds. This is why Christ came to a corrupt and dying world. He came to set the captives free (Luke 4:18). Free from what? Free from the subconscious lies of unbelief." Actor Bruce Marchiano

Actor/Writer Bruce Marchiano was once asked, "Bruce, you had the privilege to play Jesus, memorizing every word of Jesus, walking through every scene of His life. What was the big revelation?" He said, "If I could submit to you one thing. And it's a thing that is treated with such trivialness. It's a thing that people tend to look at and go 'oh well, of course,' and 'let's move on to more important things.' But I would submit to you it is the most important thing. And it boils down to a little thing I've been told ever since I was old enough to hear. But then I'm too busy living life; I don't pay attention to it, or familiarity breeds complacency, I don't know, there are other things. The big revelation. The nut of it all. The core of it all. The thing that is toughest of all to accept. He loves you. He loves you. He loves you just the way you are. You don't have to prove yourself. You don't have to impress somebody. He gave his life for you, just the way you are."

NOTABLES:

If you struggle believing Satan has been hard at work minimizing the prevalence of God in our society, realize much of the history you have learned in school has been intentionally altered. To learn more about this, there is a real cool book called *Deceived; The Assault of Revisionist History* by Keith Hoar. Mr. Hoar does an incredible job of chronicling the erosion of America's morals and values since the 1960's. He also shows us where

Satan has misled students to believe our nation's roots were never Judeo-Christian.

For more compelling data on the rise and fall of abortion in the United States, see Randall K. O'Bannon, PhD. *Out of the Long Dark Night,* 2003. https://www.nrlc.org/archive/news/2003/NRL01/randy.html

Did you know until the 1880s, United States Supreme Court Justices used the Bible and more specifically the book of Leviticus to rule on constitutional law?

Assignment: Make a sign out of 8.5 X 11 inch paper. On it write, "You Are About to Enter the Mission Field," then place it on the back of your bedroom door.

2

THE STRONGHOLD OF SATAN: FALSE BELIEF

Following this I saw another Angel descend from Heaven. His authority was immense, his glory flooded earth with Brightness, his voice thunderous: "`Ruined, ruined, Great Babylon, ruined! A ghost town for demons is all that's left!"

Revelation 18:1-2 MSG

For though we live in the world, we do not wage war as the world does. The weapons we fight with are not the weapons of the world. On the contrary, they have divine power to demolish strongholds.

2 Corinthians 10:3-5 NIV

I have given you authority to trample on snakes and scorpions and to overcome all the power of the enemy; nothing will harm you. However, do not rejoice that the spirits submit to you, but rejoice your names are written in heaven.

Luke 10:19-20 NIV

The city of Corinth was a booming metropolis of its day situated along the Corinthian isthmus of the Mediterranean Sea. This Greek city had two harbors and was a hub for world commerce. Many traveled through this city and brought with them the cultural beliefs of their land. For this reason, Corinth was known to be multicultural, and polytheistic (serving many pagan gods). One such god, Aphrodite, fostered prostitution in the name of religion bringing with it mass immorality and corruption. At one time, over 1,000 sacred prostitutes served in her temple.

A heavy demonic influence existed over this city making the early Christian church powerless to reach the lost. Many young Christians were feeling the oppression of these demonic strongholds when witnessing the good news of Jesus Christ. The Apostle Paul recognized this and was compelled, not once but twice in just a few months, to write these young Christians (1 & 2 Corinthians), urging them to stand against the worldly beliefs that were infiltrating their way into the Christian church. He referred to these beliefs within the mind as strongholds of the enemy.

Thank God those letters found their way into your Bible, because Christians of today live in much the same conditions as that of the early church in Corinth. Just as the church in Corinth was plagued with numerous demonic problems, so too do we find worldly beliefs infiltrating their way into the church in America. If we are to use the Apostle Paul's advice, then it is important we understand what these weapons are, and how we can use them to pull down the demonic strongholds of the enemy.

The Greek word for stronghold means fortress or castle. In Biblical times, a fortress or castle was built with high walls to protect the people that lived within them. Unfortunately, that which initially was used to protect could also be used to imprison. Often, the typical strategy of war against a fortress or castle was to surround it and keep food and supplies from reaching the people within. What was once intended to protect now binds. Spiritual fortresses exist in our "thought patterns" and "ideas" and do much the same thing.

Information stored at the subconscious level develops the attitudes and beliefs we live by. Beliefs are either built on truth or lie. There is nothing in between. Half-truths and little white lies are nothing more than a lie with a subtle tinge of truth to them. Often these lies are hard to unveil (1 Corinthians 13:12 NIV), a deception subtly put in place by the enemy to produce suffering. Most are developed when we are most impressionable which is from birth to age eight. Our parents play a huge role in the development of our belief system.

The first time I heard the words "demonic stronghold," I couldn't help but think of it as some wrestling move demons use to pin us down. For the most part, that is what a demonic stronghold is; a belief of the mind that pins us down and holds us back from having what God wants for our lives. In 2 Corinthians 10:5 (NIV), the Apostle Paul establishes to the church what these strongholds are: arguments and every pretension (false beliefs) that set themselves up against the knowledge of God (truth).

This makes perfect sense if you are to step back and look at the war for your soul. God has made it very clear; we, His children, must first believe in order to be saved (Mark 16:16; Acts 16:31; Romans 10:9). By infiltrating lies and false beliefs into our minds at such a young age, Satan can stop us from believing we are loved by our Creator just the way we are.

Though many demonic strongholds may plague us, they tend to fall into four categories. They are: 1) I must meet certain standards to feel loved or accepted. 2) I must be approved of by certain people in my life to feel loved or accepted. 3) If I fail, I don't deserve to be loved or accepted and should be punished. And 4) I am who I am. I cannot change. I am hopeless.

Let's look at an example of each to give you a taste of how these false beliefs play out in our lives.

Driven

An example of a person who falls prey to the stronghold of false belief "I must meet certain standards to feel loved or accepted" is a young man named Jack. Jack is the starting quarterback of his high school football team, the starting point guard of his high school basketball team, and the starting pitcher for his high school baseball team. Likewise, he carries a 4.5 GPA in school and is seriously being recruited as a quarterback from universities like Notre Dame, Michigan, and USC.

No matter what Jack does, he is driven to win. On the other hand, Jack seriously struggles with losing and more importantly, dealing with the "incompetence" of his teammates. He knows that his ability to get into a university rely on his teammates doing their job. Jack's parents, teachers, and coaches all love Jack because Jack seems to excel in whatever he does. Jack finds some things like sports come natural to him. Other things like schoolwork do not. He has a strong work ethic and believes anything he tries can be conquered if he puts in the work. So, he stays up late to keep his grades up. Simply put, nothing is going to stop Jack from realizing his dream of one day playing in the NFL.

Since Jack was a boy, his father, an ex-Marine and successful high school athlete once, swore to raise Jack to be successful as well. He regimented Jack's life. After school, Jack was on club teams practicing. When he got home, he wasn't allowed to play with his friends. Instead, he was sent to his room to study. Jack's father continually explained that this is how the "successful" kids lived and if Jack wanted to be "successful," he had to put in the time.

Jack's father was his biggest fan. He would video tape Jack's games and sit down with Jack afterward and point out what Jack could do to get better. When Jack excelled in the classroom or on the playing field, his dad was the first to congratulate him reminding Jack that his hard work was paying off. And when Jack messed up, he was disciplined. His father would lecture him of the need to constantly be striving for perfection. It hinged on verbal, emotional, and sometimes physical abuse.

Jack's mind is full of confidence and pride. He tells himself, "I don't care what it takes, I'm going to win. I have what it takes. No one can stop me." On the subconscious level, his thoughts sound different. "I have to succeed. If I don't, I'm a nobody, a loser." The false belief Satan has on Jack's mind is, "I must meet certain standards to feel loved or accepted."

Making the Grade

As a young Asian student, Darren finds himself being compared to his older brother who found school easy and enjoyable. His brother's dream and the dream of his parents is to obtain a Genetic Engineering degree on a full-ride scholarship to prestigious Stanford University. He boasted someday he would be the one to cure cancer. Unfortunately, Darren, a high school junior, has no idea what he wants to do in life. Both his mother and father know the value of education and the advantage it brings.

Darren's father demands Darren take AP courses and places education as a priority in life. He doesn't allow Darren to play an instrument in the band or participate in any after-school activities. Darren works hard to please his father as it is part of his culture. He strives to make the grades, but with no clear understanding of what he wants to do with his life, he continually falls short of his father's clear expectations. His father is constantly on him, and any time Darren sits down to do his AP Calculus, he has an overwhelming desire to play online video games instead.

Darren is plagued with thoughts of inadequacy. "What's the use? I'll never be like my older brother. I'll be lucky to get into a community college." Soon Darren finds comfort in smoking weed with his friends. Keeping it hidden from his parents and trying to meet the expectations of his father, Darren sees his life spinning out of control and confusing. His grades begin to fall. His father rides him even harder, telling him he will be a nobody if he doesn't excel in school. This reinforces the lie living deep within his mind which is, "I must be approved of by certain people (ie. my father) in my life to feel loved or accepted."

Plagued by Anxiety

Susan was one of three children being raised in a conditionally loving home by a single mother of strong German descent. When Susan was a little girl, her father left the family never looking back. Life had been chaotic since the divorce. Her mother had to hold down two jobs to make ends meet. There was little time for playing. On Saturdays, her older sister and younger brother were asked to do chores. If they did not do them to her mother's standards, they were reprimanded. Conversely, if they did them to her mother's liking, they were praised for their effort.

Susan would labor in vain to have her bed made perfectly and her room cleaned perfectly, and all the rest of her chores done perfectly as to avoid any reprimand from mom. Problem was, until mom inspected her work, she did not know if she met her mother's expectations. As Susan grew, so did the expectations. In middle school, she was asked to cook dinner and wash the dishes while her mom caught up on work. By the time she was in high school, Susan was expected to work a part-time job to help make ends meet, keep the house clean, and cook the nights she didn't work all while keeping a 4.0 grade point average. If she did not keep up to her mother's standards, punishment often in the form of guilt and shame ensued. Upon inspection, her mother would snap, "Oh my God! What are you doing? That's not how you do it. You need to..." In conversation, her mom would interrupt her at times with words like, "How could you say such a thing?" or "That's not going to work," or "Are you crazy?"

Often Susan questions herself and her abilities. She has serious anxiety when thinking of speaking in public or performing in any capacity before a crowd. Her thoughts say things like, "I can't do this. If I make a mistake, everyone will laugh at me. I'm not like my friends who like to be on stage." Often, Susan finds comfort hanging out in her room singing. She has a beautiful voice that the world will never hear because she has bought into the demonic stronghold, "If I fail, I don't deserve to be loved or accepted and should be punished."

Losing Weight

Jessica is an overweight girl who desperately wants to lose weight. On the surface, she is ready for the pounds to come off; however, growing up as a child, she was sexually molested by her Uncle. She now has subconscious thoughts that say things like, "I don't want to look attractive, because men (who are all pigs) will come on to me. I'd rather hide in an unattractive body than deal with pigs."

The dieting may start off well and the weight may start coming off, but at some point, let's say ten pounds later, these subconscious thoughts begin to sabotage her effort. She starts to hear the voices in her mind, "I'm not good enough, I'm not pretty enough, what's the use, even if I lose the weight, it will just come back on."

Finally, she caves. With her will weakened by her thoughts, she begins eating the food she has been craving for days. Her feelings of guilt and shame further exacerbate the problem. The voices continue, "Why do I even try? I know I don't have the willpower. Why can't I accept myself for who I am, fat?" The guilt and shame persist until the battle is lost. The weight begins to come back on. Now, feeling even more depressed and stuck, she gives up on herself. Never asking the question, "Why is it that I sabotage myself every time I get down to a certain weight?" she never truly understands the war being waged and its effects on her life. The demonic stronghold of false belief that Jessica doesn't even know plagues her life is the thought, "I am who I am. I cannot change. I am hopeless."

These examples were given to you to help you understand how Satan places false belief into a person's mind and why the Apostle Paul felt so strongly about telling everyone where the battle for everyone's soul is being waged. You may be saying to yourself," They look so similar, how can anyone fall into just one of these lies?" You're right. They are so subtly different that often we fall prey to more than just one. This is why it is so vitally important to discover which of these we are listening to in order to free ourselves from Satan's attack.

How Satan Reinforces His Lies

To separate us from God, Satan attacks our mind with arguments of false belief that sound so convincing and are delivered to us from our parents that we fall prey to his crafty scheme (Exodus 20:5, Numbers 14:18). Satan knows if we buy into his lie, the feelings of shame and guilt will overcome us, so he offers us an escape to help us cope with what we believe to be true. Unfortunately, chasing the escape just solidifies the false belief even more. Caught in this reinforcement loop, our hearts harden over time. Let's look back to when all this started to get an idea of what I mean.

If we look at Satan's work with Eve in the Garden, we realize step one is to fall prey to the false belief, and step two is to look for a way to cope with the emotional pain the false belief brings. This coping mechanism further separates us from the Father as we fall to the temptation to rely on ourselves and not God (what I call worshiping your idol). Eve fell prey to Satan's lie or false belief, "You surely will not die! For God knows in the day you eat from it, your eyes will be opened, and you will be like God knowing good from evil. [You will be more, have more, feel freer than ever]" (Genesis 3:4) She believed the lie and ate the fruit. The fruit was nothing more than an idol or object of worship. Eating the fruit represented taking on life under her own strength. As time has gone on, the idol has changed; Satan's plan, however, has remained the same.

The Idols of Today

When we read in the Bible about idols, they always seem to depict an object or a statue the people were worshiping (remember the golden calf and Baal). In today's world, this seems rather silly as most Christians don't place some object on their fireplace mantle and start worshiping it (Okay. Maybe if you're a Disney, NFL, or NASCAR fan you might). In their book entitled *Killing the Victim Before the Victim Kills You*, Derek M. Watson, Daniel Tocchini, and Larry Pinci write of how Satan has devised four clever yet subtle idols that have pervaded the Christian world. They call these idols gods that all of us worship in one form or another. They are the idols of **looking good, feeling good, being right, and being comfortable**. These idols become like medicine to stop the pain of Satan's stronghold so deeply embedded within our subconscious. Like medicine, the idols are what we worship to manage the psychological pain of the false belief. In doing so, however, we, like Eve, become reliant on ourselves and not God.

Now if you find this kind of weird, it gets even weirder. Each idol appeals to a different lie. Those who want to **look good** are usually plagued with the stronghold "I must meet certain standards to feel loved or accepted." Those who want to **feel good** are plagued by "I must be approved of by certain people in my life to feel loved or accepted." Those who want to **be right** are plagued by the stronghold "If I fail, I don't deserve to be loved or accepted and should be punished." And those who are creatures of **comfort** and hate conflict are plagued with the stronghold, "I am who I am, I cannot change, I am hopeless."

Now all we have to do is take notice of the idol which is on the surface to understand the stronghold of Satan which lies deep within the recesses of our mind. This sets us up to reach into the heart of another in a way that is serving to God. It also allows the truth to take root in one's mind.

The Stronghold of God: Humility

The hardest person you will ever get to know is yourself.

John Savage

Our unawareness allows strongholds of false belief to continue to keep us under their spell. Because they exist within our subconscious thought life, they are difficult to detect. However, they are usually quite evident to our closest friends and family. Often, we need the help of these friends who care enough about us to be honest.

Francis Frangipane, in his book entitled *The Three Battlegrounds* writes:

A demonic stronghold is any type of thinking that exalts itself above the *knowledge* of God, thereby giving the devil a secure place of influence in an individual's thought life.

In most cases, we are not talking about 'spirit possession.' This author does not believe that a Christian can be possessed, for when a person is 'possessed' by a demon, that demon fills their spirit the way the Holy Spirit fills the spirit of a Christian.

However, Christians can be *oppressed* by demons, which can occupy unregenerate thought-systems, especially if those thoughts are defended by self-deception or false doctrines! The thought, 'I cannot have a demon because I am a Christian' is simply untrue. A demon cannot have you in an eternal, possessive sense, but you can *have a demon* if you refuse to repent of your sympathetic thoughts toward evil. Your rebellion toward God provides a place for the devil in your life.

Now to think, "If I fail, I don't deserve to be loved and should be punished," is pure foolishness. My refusal to repent of this **sympathetic thought towards evil** allows the stronghold to strengthen. The truth is, I was created to love and be loved (Jeremiah 29:11; Ephesians 1:3-14). Every time I buy into this deception and chase the idol, I **defend** what simply isn't true or working in my life. And every time I defend what isn't true or working in my life, I **reinforce** the false belief or stronghold that binds me. Defend, reinforce. Defend, reinforce. Over and over again. This reinforcement hardens my heart over time. Soon, I find myself wondering if life will ever change.

For some reason, I have an overwhelming tendency to defend my shortcomings as if I can persuade another into believing they aren't there. What I'm defending is my unrighteousness. However hard I work to justify my actions, I know the accusation placed before me has some truth to it. This is why Jesus said, "Settle matters quickly with your adversary [enemy]..." or "Agree with thine adversary quickly... "(Mathew 5:25 KJV). Satan is my adversary. By quickly admitting to the lie of false belief that dwells in my heart, I will do the exact thing that will cause him to flee.

Hey, let's face it, all of us are as filthy as rags (Isaiah 64:6). A kid who steps into a mud puddle cannot clean himself. We all need a Savior! This is the very reason we have compassion on those who have yet to know Him. The quicker we come to realize Jesus alone is our righteousness, the quicker our adversary, the devil, will lose his stronghold within our minds. Mr. Frangipane goes on to write, "The strength of humility is that it builds a spiritual defense around your soul, prohibiting strife, competition, and many of life's irritations from stealing your peace."

Until I humble myself and admit I have strongholds, I will continue to stay stuck in life. Remember, a stronghold of unbelief is a dwelling place within the dark recesses of my mind. My unwillingness to humble myself before another and admit I'm not perfect is a direct result of pride. And what do Satan and his demons think of humility? According to Mr. Frangipane, "Satan fears virtue. He is terrified of humility; he hates it. He sees a humble person and it sends chills down his back. His hair stands up when Christians kneel down, for humility is the surrender of the soul to God." This is the key to bringing down any stronghold of false doctrine: **virtue and humility**.

Every time a close friend or family member criticizes me for a shortcoming (being insensitive, arrogant, critical, right all the time, etc.), I stop. Listen to what they are saying. I then look for the stronghold of unbelief that prompts me to be this way. Instead of responding by defending myself, which could easily escalate into an argument, I quickly agree with them. More times than not their experience of me has some semblance of truth to it. Then, after I've received the criticism, I **humble** myself and admit, in all sincerity, what they are saying is true. I explain to them I've struggled with this before and see it as the work of Satan in my life. Then, I take it to the next level. I ask them to pray with me right then and there to release my mind from the stronghold that binds me in unbelief (fear of failure, fear of rejection, fear of unacceptance, or fear of hopelessness). This is the kind of humility God is looking for. By doing this one simple act, I live in a love and acceptance I've never experienced before.

In the next chapter, we'll add one more layer to this truth and look at how a person's personality affects the lie they listen to and the idol they chase. Now get with your mentor to discuss this chapter. He or she may have a challenge for you, so be ready? May the force be with you.

QUOTABLES:

The Arena

Listen to this quote given by a famous President back in 1910:

"It is not the critic who counts; not the man who points out how the strong man stumbles or where the doer of deeds could have done better. The credit belongs to the man who is actually in the arena, whose face is marred by dust and sweat and blood, who strives valiantly, who errs and comes up short again and again, because there is no effort without error or shortcoming, but who knows the great enthusiasms, the great devotions, who spends himself for a worthy cause; who, at the best, knows, in the end, the triumph of high achievement, and who, at the worst, if he fails, at least he fails while daring greatly, so that his place shall never be with those cold and timid souls who knew neither victory nor defeat."

President Theodore Roosevelt

What is your arena? Is it sports or the performing arts? Maybe it's academics or livestock. Regardless, President Roosevelt is saying, "Recognize your effort, not the results, for that is where your reward is. As long as you are stepping out and fighting the good fight, that is what turns you into a champion."

When I was younger, I used to rock climb. I've come to realize life is much like rock climbing; if I want to succeed I have to let go of one hold to reach for the next, and in between, there is a chance I may fall. In the world of finance, it is called Risk/Reward. In order to make money, I have to risk my own hard-earned money. The chance I may fail in my investment is just as great as success. The only way I will risk is if I'm willing to give up what I have for something better. This "daring greatly," as President Roosevelt calls it, is what propels me in life. If I'm not willing to "dare greatly" and give up what I have, I can't move forward (just play a game of Monopoly, and you'll know exactly what I'm talking about).

NOTABLES:

Did you know most people fear success more so than failure? Why is that? There may be many reasons, but the one I fall prey to is success draws the attention of the public eye. That's right; people take notice. Now, I must take on a greater responsibility of meeting these people's expectations (or at least what I think are their expectations). They will expect more of me than I can offer. They will see me for who I am, not an expert, just a common man. It is better to blend in with the crowd than to face the chance I may lose my success (remember the parable of talents). This uncomfortable feeling stops me from taking bold moves to be who God intended me to be. To save me from these feelings, a small voice rears up within the deep recesses of my subconscious. "I can't have that, I don't have what it takes!" or "Even if I did get what I wanted, I wouldn't be responsible enough to keep it. Others will be watching me just waiting to point out what I already know to be true; I'm not good enough to have this!" (Good enough can be replaced with important enough, smart enough, strong enough, tough enough, handsome enough, talented enough, etc.)

Soon these subconscious arguments begin to hem me in. Even if I look deep within, my natural reaction is to cower from the idea I really can change. So, I go back to the "familiar" no matter how painful it may be. This is why some women stay stuck in abusive relationships, and why others don't even attempt to lose weight. **It's the strongholds of unbelief that keep us stuck in life.**

According to Child Psychologist, Dr. Kevin Leman, children raised in homes where they are judged by their performance often cower from activities or projects that will bring criticism from others. The shame of not "measuring up" debilitates them. Often, they won't even try new things or take new risks because they've rehearsed in their brain arguments and reasons why they won't succeed.

Conversely, children raised in a home where parents teach excellence, rather than performance, welcome criticism. They aren't reprimanded if they don't perform. Instead, their parents ask them questions like "Did you do everything you could to prepare for this? How could you have prepared differently? Is there another way that may be better?" It is the learning process that is praised, not the results.

Notes:

Stronghold: I must meet certain standards to feel loved or accepted
Idol: Looking Good

Stronghold: I must be approved of by certain people in my life to feel loved or accepted.
Idol: Feeling Good

Stronghold: If I fail, I don't deserve to be loved or accepted and should be punished.
Idol: Being Right

Stronghold: I am who I am. I cannot change. I am hopeless.
Idol: Being Comfortable

3

DIVINE SECRETS

Oh yes, you shaped me first inside, then out; you formed me in my mother's womb. I thank you, High God—you're breathtaking! Body and soul, I am marvelously made! I worship in creation—what a creation! You know me inside and out, you know every bone in my body; You know exactly how I was made bit by bit, how I was sculpted from nothing into something. Like an open book, you watched me grow from conception to birth; all the stages of my life were spread out before you, the days of my life all prepared before I'd even lived one day... Investigate my life O God, find out everything about me; cross-examine and test me, get a clear picture of what I'm about; see for yourself whether I've done anything wrong—then guide me on the road to eternal life.

Psalm 139:13-16 & 23-24 (MSG)

Do not be deceived: God is not mocked; for whatever a man sows, this he will also reap. For the one who sows to his own flesh will from the flesh reap corruption, but the one who sows to the Spirit will from the Spirit reap eternal life.

Galatians 6:7-8

Only a life lived for others is a life worthwhile.

Albert Einstein

And the disciples came and said to Him, "Why do You speak to them in parables?" Jesus answered them, "To you it has been granted to know the mysteries of the kingdom of heaven, but to them, it has not been granted."

Matthew 13:10-11

Don't you find it somewhat odd that Jesus would use parables to deliver His message to the world? It really doesn't make sense. Why would someone, who had a message for the world to hear, speak in code? If I were Him, I'd want everyone to understand what I was trying to say. I'd speak as plainly as I possibly could. Yet Jesus has defined His reason in Matthew 13:11 (see also John 8:43). He calls those who are able to decipher the code as those who are able to know the mysteries of the kingdom of God. These mysteries are what I call Divine Secrets.

Like riddles, parables are word puzzles designed to get those that can decode them to see a bigger possibility. The Bible is full of riddles. If you die once you live twice, but if you die twice you only live once. Huh? These secrets give us power when used against the evil of our day. If used in accordance with God's will, they can literally create revival in your school. If used out of God's will, they will cause destruction in your life and the lives of others. In his book, *Youth Aflame*, Winkie Pratney writes of these Divine Secrets as the learning of God's supernatural powers. Being a superhero for God, however, comes with a price. Listen to what Winkie writes:

Learning supernatural powers are not the most important thing; what is *really* important is to be the kind of person God can trust with His secrets. That is why God puts so much stress on our holy walk in this world. It would be wrong for God to share His powers with a selfish person. Think of all the damage they could do to the Universe! Satan's *first temptation* to Adam and Eve was to urge them into trying powers they were not yet mature enough to handle. The devil still captures men by the same suggestion – '*You* shall be as *god.*' (Genesis 3:5) God will never 'bribe' men into serving Him. He does not respond to selfish appeals from sinners for power or control over others with forces that ordinary people do not have.

The first secret we are going to discover is the secret of Selflessness. It may not seem so Divine, but when used in accordance to God's will, it is one of the strongest Supernatural Powers you will ever use. Selflessness means to forgo my own wants and needs for the wants and needs of others. To begin understanding this secret we must work to understand who people are. By getting a general awareness of others personalities, we will be better suited to serve. Please realize this is where we begin and not where we end. Understanding a person's unique personality is not a way to label them, but instead a way to understand why they say what they say and do what they do. So, let's get started.

Personality

You possess in your individuality certain unseen, unique, and intangible properties. Your reputation, taste in music, likes and dislikes, imagination, ability to think freely, memory, and the ability to tap into your conscience are but just a few things that make up your character. We call these unseen, unique, and intangible properties our personality. It truly defines who you are. Like a snowflake or fingerprint, no other person on this earth has your personality. When God carved you into existence, He gave you this personality to use for His glory. It is another way God shows us how precious and special we are.

Much of our personality is modeled to us through our parents. If you think about it, you are just a younger version of your mom and dad. Some of you may be thinking, "But I don't want to be like my mom and dad." Think again, look at all the awesome qualities you possess. Where do you think you got them? I'm sure if you look hard enough, you'd find them in your mom or dad as well. I love my dad's humor, and my mom's desire to do things right and just. It's important to remember your parents aren't perfect. Yes, they do have faults that may make them hard to live with at times, but so do you. We all fall short of perfection (Romans 3:23).

If you can't see any good qualities in your parents, you may want to look at the un-forgiveness you have toward them. I suggest you stop reading, clear your mind, and write down when and how your parents may have hurt you. Then pray to God and ask him to forgive you for harboring these feelings toward your mom or dad. Honestly, this un-forgiveness is killing you, not them. If you can't seem to forgive them, get with your mentor and talk about it. You will be surprised at the healing powers this brings.

Everyone's personality is divided into strengths and weaknesses. Strengths are those qualities I possess that draw me closer to those I love and am in relationship with. Weaknesses, on the other hand, are those qualities I possess that seem to drive people away. It's my junk, my baggage, my sin, the stuff I carry in life that I don't want to carry. The stuff that if I don't deal with, my wife, my family, and my friends end up having to deal with. My weaknesses are the result of those strongholds Satan has worked so hard to place into my subconscious.

It is important for me to know the strengths and weaknesses I carry if I am going to want to grow. Think about it. If I am being commanded to love my neighbor as myself, then I have to understand myself first before I can understand my neighbor. God calls me to pull the log out of my eye before I am to pull the sawdust out of my friend's eye (Matthew 7:1-5). What is revealed when I take the time to humbly look within, is the reality of who I am. "Then you will know the truth and the truth will set you free." (John 8:32)

The problem for many of us, including our friends, is that we are scared to admit we have faults or shortcomings. Built into our very being, God has created an overwhelming desire for us to love and be loved. This gnawing hunger in our hearts drives us to insulate ourselves from what we know isn't working in our lives in order to protect ourselves from the unacceptance of others. We fear the potential judgments and alienation of our peers. So, we cover up our faults as best we can. Now here lies the problem; shielding ourselves from truth does not protect love—it suffocates it. Being preserved deep within the recesses of our mind is the stronghold of Satan. "I am not good enough to be loved." This is what Daniel Tocchini calls "exchanging the short-term pain of the truth for emotional comfort."

You see this all the time in dating relationships. Believe it or not, we all put our best foot forward when we begin dating someone. We look charming, witty, humorous, positive, expressive, self-confident, energetic, and fun. Never do we reveal our weaknesses and talk about past sins, hurts, and/or failures. Steeped deep within our mind is the fear that if we did, "that person wouldn't want to be with me." So, we play someone we are not, hoping the image we portray will be good enough. As time passes, we find it harder and harder to hold onto the ideal person we've put on to be. Soon we become imprisoned to the fear that we have to be the person we are not in order to be liked or loved.

Although truth may be uncomfortable at first, it does set one free. Listen to the words Mr. Tocchini writes in his book *Killing the Victim Before the Victim Kills You.*

> Reality has a wonderful quality about it—it doesn't care how you feel or what you think. It makes no bones about being brutally honest. You never need to worry whether reality is coddling you with half-truths. No matter what your opinion is of any subject, reality is true to itself. Rocks are hard, and water is wet. Even if you think and wish it to be different, rocks are not velvet and water is not dry. Reality is what it is.

All relationships that start off where one reveals only the good side of themselves end in betrayal. Why? Because the **reality** of who we are and the junk we carry will eventually show up. The person receiving the **reality** feels slighted as they begin to experience the good, the bad and the ugly of this other person.

Let's go back to our dating analogy. How many times have you heard a friend tell you it just didn't work out because the person they were dating totally changed and became a jerk or a witch? I ask you;

did they really change or did the **reality** of who they are surface in the relationship?

It is imperative as followers of Christ to humble ourselves and look at our reality; to readily admit in humility to our closest friends our imperfections and ask them to help us free ourselves from this "sin" or stronghold that binds us. Timing is everything, so in the coming chapters I'll teach you when is the right time to ask your friends to help you overcome your bad and ugly. By doing so your vulnerability will open deeper levels of communication and authenticity with your friends. Then you won't have to go around wondering if your friends are going to find you out. Maybe for the first time in your life you will experience the freedom of being accepted for who you are.

Remember, Satan fears virtue and is terrified of humility. He cannot work with those who are virtuous and humble. He has no way in, no pride to hang his hat on. It is humility that unbinds us from the underlying strongholds of unbelief in our lives. He is terrified of what would happen if we could expose the strongholds that lie within our subconscious. For our weapons of warfare are of **divine power** to demolish strongholds. These are the very strongholds that we war against.

Jesus, the Perfect Model

Jesus was the perfect model. He was what all of us who are called Christian (like Christ) aspire to be. His personality was full of strengths. He had no weakness. He had no strongholds of false belief; therefore, He had no bad or ugly parts of His personality. Simply put, He was without sin (2 Corinthians 5:21; Hebrews 4:15). What He did have was compassion for those who were being tormented by these strongholds of false belief. He so deeply desired to see them freed from the lies they were listening to. If we truly desire to be like Him, we must take on the same attitude (Ephesians 4:22-24). His vision, to "set the captives free" (Luke 4:18) was a vision big enough to live for! It was also a vision big enough to die for!

The first step in discovering these strongholds is the hardest. It requires an honest look at ourselves (James 1:24-25 MSG), an inventory of the strengths and weaknesses we carry. Remember, God calls us to take the log out of our eye before we are to take the speck of sawdust out of our friend's eye (Luke 6:41-42).

Now let's get started in looking at the good and bad of four distinct personalities that all of us seem to carry. They will equip you to see your friends in a way you've never seen them before, and in so doing, you'll be able to understand the strongholds Satan has on their life.

The Lion, Otter, Beaver, and Golden Retriever

Understanding people is the key to understanding their strongholds. In the world of acting, there is a saying: "If you get to the 'why,' you get to the character's heart." If you want to really get to know your friends, you'll have to ask the question "Why?" Understanding why they do what they do will tell you a lot about the condition of their heart. That is all Jesus did—he went right to the heart. Read of the Samaritan woman at the well, the woman with the issue of blood, the rich young ruler, the leper, the Centurion, the blind man, the Pharisees and Sadducees, Nicodemus, Mary and Martha, and you'll experience Jesus speaking right into the heart of His children. He served them in love by tenderly and not so tenderly exposing the strongholds of Satan in their minds. He calls you and I to do the same.

As I have alluded to before, we are all unique and wonderfully made by our Creator. Although there have never been two snowflakes alike, they are all made up of the same ingredients—hydrogen, and oxygen. Like DNA, God in His infinite wisdom has never allowed two of the same persons to walk on the face of this earth; however, the basic ingredients for our personality can be divided into four types as outlined by Dr. Gary Smalley, PhD and Dr. John Trent, PhD. Each has its very own unique strengths and weakness. Doctors. Smalley and Trent call these four personalities the Lion, the Otter, the Beaver, and the Golden Retriever.

We all hold within us various percentages of these personality traits, so a lion does have some Golden Retriever and a Beaver has some Otter in him or her. According to Dr. Smalley, we usually find that one or two of these traits dominate our personality. Also, Dr. Smalley goes on to say, the goal for you and I or any Christian, for that matter, is to develop the strengths of all four of these personality types while diminishing the weaknesses.

The Lion

In the wilds of Africa, the beast that stands above all beasts is the lion. He is at the top of the food chain and has dominion over all his wild kingdom except the elephant (It's cool cause lions don't eat elephants and elephants don't eat lions). Someone who has the personality type of a lion is very much a leader. Alexander the Great, Napoleon, Thomas Jefferson, Abraham Lincoln, Charles Darwin, Dwight D. Eisenhower, General Douglas MacArthur, Vince Lombardi, Margaret Thatcher, Steve Jobs, Dave Ramsey, and President Donald Trump are but a few of the lions we've seen or see in the world today. King Saul, the apostle Paul, the Roman Centurion, Nicodemus, the Pharisees and Sadducees are but a few Biblical characters that were once lions. Five to seven percent of those that go to your school are predominantly lion.

The Lion's Strengths:

These are the movers and shakers of society. Their personality strengths include commanding authority and taking charge of situations when no one else does. They are highly motivated, determined, confident, and firm. They're enterprising, always looking for opportunity to enhance themselves and others. They enjoy challenges and tend to want to solve the world's problems. Their mind is always thinking about ways to do things better. They are incredibly efficient and productive with their time, never seeming to rest or relax. They consider themselves to be highly responsible. They size things up quickly, then dive in. They tend to want to get involved with every school project and function you can think of. They are quick to make decisions, and bold in carrying them out. They live life with purpose, rarely playing for enjoyment. They must have a reason why they do what they do. They are intuitive and visionary, often seeing things before anyone else. They are also goal driven planners; they schedule everything. They are adventurous and have an incredibly strong work ethic. These are the people who tend to compete in the Olympics or climb Mount Everest dedicating years of training for one moment of glory. They are self-reliant and action oriented. They tend to work in excellence, doing more than what others would say is necessary. They are intense, tenacious, and optimistic everything is going to work out as planned. They are logical and objective in their thinking, often asking why when they don't understand. They are respected, practical, truthful, and honest. They can be blatantly confrontational. They are motivated and know how to motivate others. Finally, because of their leadership skill, they work best when leading a team and delegating authority.

The Lion's Weaknesses:

With these strengths, however, come weaknesses. Of all the personality types, they tend to get the worst rap. Many have a hard time being in relationship with lions because they can be so blatantly honest and direct without regard for another's feelings. The term "hardnosed" undoubtedly was used to describe a lion. They also tend to be pushy and overbearing. Under pressure they can become dictatorial and loud often using intimidation to get control of the situation. They have a hard time shifting in mid-stream. Once their mind is set on a certain way of doing things, they tend to be resistant to other possibilities. They are the kid who takes his ball and goes home if everyone doesn't play what he wants to play. They have such a strong competitive spirit.

Although they love to assume leadership positions and delegate authority, they tend to become controlling of others when involved on a team. Because of the high positions they hold, they often feel entitled to special privileges. They can be relentless and cutthroat in their actions. Their ability to act in excellence can easily fall to perfectionism, not allowing others who they may work with or in relationship with the freedom to express themselves. They can be relentless in their pursuit of success often overworking themselves and expecting others to do the same. They are busy all the time, often overbooking their calendar. They can be insensitive to the needs of others often brushing people off with the excuse they don't have time (the Rabbi and Levite priest in the story of the Good Samaritan were lions, Luke 10:30-37). Sarcasm is often their form of humor. They can be un-loyal to their friends and family, betraying them at any cost to get their way. They can be prideful and independent. Also, they have been described as strong willed, stubborn, inconsiderate, cold, calculating, distant, arrogant, and openly critical. Finally, they just don't know when to or how to relax.

The Underlying Stronghold of False Belief That Binds:

What sits at the bottom of a dominant lion is the false belief: **I must meet certain standards to feel loved.** More than anything, **lions must achieve in order to feel respected.** It is for this reason they work incredibly hard to hold important positions in life. They must meet certain standards to feel good about themselves. **This false belief results in a fear of failure** although they never would admit it. Their idol, the pagan god they serve in this world, is **"looking good."** This looking good is in the form of image. They strive to have, hold and achieve the best the world has to offer. They drive the nicest cars, live in the biggest homes, and work in the most prestigious buildings. They strive for acceptance through achievement. After all, if they can become someone everyone else looks up to, they will feel important and respected.

Lions are usually raised in a home where they have little control and/or feel devalued through physical, emotional, spiritual, economic, and/or sexual abuse. Because of this, they tend to put results over relationships. Results are safe, relationships are not. By being the leader, they can control situations and therefore avoid dealing with their lack of trust in others. If they do not become aware of the stronghold that binds them, their desire to control others can lead to physical, emotional, economic, spiritual, and/or sexual abuse, thus perpetuating the cycle of sin to their wife/husband and children. This, my friend, is exactly where Satan wants them.

How to Recognize a Lion:

They say things that are offensive yet don't seem to care if they hurt feelings.

They Roar! When the slightest bit of chaos seems apparent, they take charge with authority.

They Roar! When they do not feel important or respected by another.

They will often have a booked schedule. To see them, you'll have to schedule a time.

They are extremely focused.

They don't quit.

They work hard and play hard.

Rarely do they do anything spontaneous. They are goal driven and their schedules are set to achieve these goals well ahead of time.

They confront others especially if results are being compromised.

Rarely are they wrong.

The Otter

The otter is one of the most playful creatures in the wild. Although they live in a very dangerous environment being preyed upon by killer whales and sharks, you would never know it by the way they behave. Fear just isn't in their repertoire of feelings. Someone who has the personality of an otter is playful by nature and easy to get along with. Some famous otters include Albert Einstein, Ellen DeGeneres, Elvis Presley, General George Patton, Winston Churchill, Babe Ruth, President Ronald Reagan, Jim Carey, Dennis the Menace, Calvin and Hobbs, and Bugs Bunny. Biblical otters include: the Canaanite woman, the Apostle Peter, and King David. Thirty to forty percent of the students that go to your school have a personality that is predominately a playful otter.

The Otter's Strengths:

Like the lion, otters are people of action; however, unlike the lion, otters have no desire to achieve. A true otter appears youthful their whole life, full of energy and spontaneity. They have an overwhelming desire to be center of attention, naturally become popular, and are always the life of the party. They are always living for the moment which makes them a blast to hang with. They love to entertain and have a vivid sense of humor. They love to laugh, and their laughter is infectious. They are always looking for adventure and are willing at a moment's notice to take risks. Where a lion likes to aim then fire, otters tend to fire then aim. More times than not, because of their adventurous spontaneity, they find themselves getting into trouble. They are the friend who always accepts a dare. They love to play sports. They are some of the most playful, energetic people you will ever meet.

They are the promoters of the world. When they get a job, they gravitate toward sales positions because they love to promote, and they love the challenge of getting another to say yes. In their mind a job must be fun and adventurous. I knew a girl in high school whose summer job was as a rafting guide in Colorado. Scooping ice cream or flipping burgers just wouldn't cut it for her.

One of their biggest attributes is they are personable. They make friends easily. They have no problem striking up a conversation with a stranger; to them, that person is a potential lifelong friend. Remember, they have no fear. They are expressive, compassionate, and warm when in conversation. They tend to captivate people's attention when speaking. They are great story tellers always alluding to detail, and they love to tell jokes. They feel comfortable being the center of attention. They love to entertain. After meeting an otter, you feel you've known them forever. They are not afraid to be emotional, yet usually tend to be happy all the time. When asked pertinent questions, they are quick to respond leaving you wondering if they just know everything or they know how to lie their way through anything.

Otters are positive people. Much like the lion, they can visualize things well, often quickly solving problems for others, however they have no desire to be recognized for it. Of all the personalities, the otter adapts to any situation well. They simply "roll with the punches," never seeming to notice the reality of their situation. Words that describe the otter are: enthusiastic, motivated, risk taker, energetic, talkative, fun loving, a promoter, friendly, mixes easily, popular, happy all the time, positive, expressive, outgoing, etc.

I just wonder how many otters have been misdiagnosed with ADHD.

The Otter's Weaknesses:

Because of their overwhelming desire to be the center of attention, otters tend to over commit themselves. They will commit to three different friends doing three different things on a Saturday night because the next thing sounds so much more fun. They tend to break promises with regularity, oblivious to the consequences of their actions. They seem to live life in a reactive mode, playing a victim to their circumstances. They can be labeled as irresponsible, undependable, a goof off, disloyal, undisciplined, impulsive, narcissistic, and foolish. They tend to shy away from deep intimate relationships, causing them to seem superficial. They often attack others with sarcastic remarks not realizing the pain they are causing (this is usually followed up with an "I was just kidding" when they realize the hurt they've caused).

They can be impatient and restless and bore easily. They are free spirited and have difficulty finishing the projects they start, including school. They find it difficult submitting to authority—faculty, staff, parents, etc. Often, they take pride in their freelance lifestyle. They can be impulsive and unstable. They tend to run from their problems. They can walk away—from their family, a relationship, a job, a team, a club faster than anyone else without thinking of the consequences they may face because of it. Although they can connect with you when you first meet them, they are rarely serious and have difficulty engaging in intimate conversation. You may feel ripped off after being in a relationship with one of them for a while. Rarely do they plan, budget their money or their time. They are not detail oriented. They forget when homework is due and have no idea what a calendar is. They tend to be flirtatious giving others the wrong impression. Finally, they tend to be weak willed, often saying yes when they know it would be best to say no. This sets them up for compulsivity—gambling, doing drugs, sex, pornography, etc.

The Underlying Stronghold of False Belief That Binds:

What sits at the bottom of a dominant otter is the false belief: **I must be approved of by certain people in my life to feel loved.** Unless they sense approval from certain people in their life, they tend to shy away from the gift they are. **This false belief results in a fear of rejection.** It is for this reason they work so hard at becoming everyone's favorite friend. Nothing aspires to their self-esteem more than the value they get from a friend saying, "you are so cool," or an authority figure saying, "good job." Their idol, the pagan god they serve in this world, is **"feeling good."** By placing themselves in positions where they can always feel good, they never have to get in touch with the pain and discomfort of their own personal rejection of "not being good enough." Since they do not approve of themselves, they turn to their peers for approval. They strive to be liked rather than respected. To demand respect would be to place themselves in a vulnerable position of not being accepted.

They are usually raised in a home where they are rarely acknowledged and feel devalued through neglect. Because of this, they tend to shy away from intimate relationships. They so desperately want to feel good enough, yet because of the neglect they felt when young, they are afraid to let people see them for who they are. The fear is who they are won't be good enough, thereby reinforcing the pain of rejection. By staying in a playful mood, they avoid emotional pain and discomfort. Remember, their idol is **feeling good**. Unfortunately, they do not realize this invulnerability ultimately drives others away. As a parent, if they do not become aware of the stronghold that binds them, their unwillingness to be intimate with their children leads to feelings of unacceptance and neglect in their children, thus perpetuating the cycle of sin to the next generation. This, my friend, is exactly where Satan wants them.

How to Recognize an Otter:

They are always playing and having fun.

You never know when they are joking or serious.

They rarely back down from a dare.

They forget the promises they make to you.

They don't have a calendar and think those that do are crazy.

It is hard to get them to commit to an opinion.

They forget names.

The Beaver

Did you know beavers spend countless hours preparing a den for their family? All of their preparation is purposed to defend their offspring from potential predators. Someone who has the personality of the beaver seems to never rest, always busying themselves. Famous beavers include Wolfgang Amadeus Mozart, Michelangelo, and Robert

Oppenheimer. Some Biblical characters that were beavers include: Martha, the apostles Mathew, Luke, and Thomas. The beaver is the richest of the four personality types, having much more to offer the world than the other three. Between forty to forty-five percent of the students that go to your school are predominant beavers.

The Beaver's Strengths:

To put it plainly, beavers are sensible people. They rarely do anything on a hunch. It must first make sense, then they just do it. Likewise, they are incredibly responsible, holding to the promises they make. The beaver has deep emotional needs for responsibility, stability, order, and tradition. By nature, they are the servants of society.

They are analytical, self-sacrificing, and sensitive to those around them. Much like beavers in the wild, everything needs to be in its place for a beaver to relax. They have a natural tendency to listen to their conscience, always looking to do right and never wanting to do wrong. They are loyal, faithful, and polite to their friends; never pushing themselves or their ideas on anyone. Once you've won over a beaver's heart, you have a friend for life.

Beavers love to be a part of volunteer groups and clubs that serve others. They hunger to contribute and rarely rest on their laurels. It is their duty to give, to care, and to serve. They feel good about themselves when they personally sacrifice for a cause greater than themselves. They are continually looking for ways to help. When playing sports, they have no problem supporting the star player on the team.

Because of their strong sense of responsibility, they are considered dependable—at home, at school, and/or at work. Rarely do they let their friends down.

They have a knack for organization and precision. They are cautious, conservative, and calculating when making decisions. Because of this, they plan well and show up prepared. They have a work ethic that puts all other personality types to shame. They are the ones that can't sleep at night if they haven't studied everything at least twice for a test the next day.

They hunger for belonging. They deeply desire to make cheer, the band, the team, or school clubs and youth group programs. It is their way of socializing and feeling like they fit in.

Beavers find status important and thrive in institutions. They love structure. They usually become government workers, doctors, accountants, and/or engineers. Most of the teachers that go to your school more than likely are beavers, because they thrive in structured learning institutions.

They are driven, always wanting more—a better grade, a better job, a better car, etc. They are incredibly hard working, and optimistic knowing if they study, practice, or work hard enough, they can improve. It is for this reason they are considered intense by their friends. Rarely do they buy junk, always owning the best quality products money can buy.

Finally, they enjoy instruction, often doing exactly what they are told. They are accurate, consistent, controlled, reserved, predictable, orderly, factual, discerning, detailed, analytical, inquisitive, precise, and persistent. Whoever said, "If it works, don't fix it," was a beaver. They rarely buck from tradition.

The Beaver's Weaknesses:

More than any other personality, dominant beavers tend to be self-centered. Like the lion, the beaver longs to be successful. They value themselves through their performance. Often, this is the reason they become the servants of society. A true beaver feels proud by what he can achieve, respected by what he can do for others, and confident through the praise he receives from others. Failure in any one of these areas sends a beaver into feelings of rejection and loneliness. When they give and give to others and/or causes and no one notices, they tend to feel disappointed and frustrated. This is what I call "Giving to Get." Their turning inward is what makes them self-centered.

What's even more wild, although they crave for external strokes to feel good about themselves, they rarely show emotion when they don't receive these strokes. Why? Because the beaver is incredibly self-conscious of their appearance. How they are being perceived by others is often in the back of their mind. Out of fear of being rejected, they forbid to look bad in the eyes of their peers, so they stuff what is really going on inside.

Because they are continually striving for acceptance through performance, they usually set unrealistic goals and standards for themselves and others. Likewise, they tend to notice what is wrong or not working. Noticing what's wrong all the time leads them to be pessimistic and critical. You do not need to criticize a beaver because more times than not, they have already criticized themselves.

Often, they see things one way, and there isn't any other way it can be done. In other words, as much as the Lion is into being right out of fear his image will suffer, the beaver is into doing right out of fear of being ridiculed. This incredible sense of duty sets them up to live in a world of "one possibility," and appear rigid, anal, intense, and serious. You will often hear them criticize another, "That's not the way you do it."

Because of their desire to do things right they spend much of their time studying for exams, practicing on the field or in the gym, and working on school projects. This time spent "over preparing" often causes performance anxiety and the feeling that they still aren't ready. After all, their worth is on the line. This gives them the appearance of being overly cautious and/or procrastinating.

Someone who has too much beaver will struggle being in loving relationships with others, because they tend to feel threatened by another's disapproval. It is difficult for a beaver to believe that another person can accept and approve of them just the way they are. The beaver also has a hard time forgiving those who've wronged them. This inability to forgive causes them to carry grudges for years. Rarely do they outwardly express their distaste to another. Instead, they seek revenge through gossip and back biting.

The Underlying Stronghold of False Belief That Binds:

What sits at the bottom of a dominant beaver's subconscious mind is the false belief: **"If I fail, I don't deserve to be loved and should be punished."** Simply put, **Beavers fear punishment.** It is for this reason they tend to fall into a performance trap. As long as they are performing to their expectations or the expectations of their parents, teachers, bosses, coaches, and peers they feel approved of and loved. They must meet these standards to feel good about themselves.

Their idol, the pagan god they serve in this world, is **"being right."** If they are right, there is no fear of punishment. So, they strive to be right and hate being wrong. Being wrong brings on guilt and shame.

Beavers are usually raised in a home where one or both parents are beavers themselves. Their parents tend to micro-manage them because that is what beavers do. This sets their parents up to feel important and approved of by their peers. This co-dependent caretaking behavior stems from the belief that my child is unable to re for themselves in this cruel world and they need my love and protection. Unfortunately, this "love and protection" shows up in the parent-child relationship as controlling with little trust their child will be able to "do anything right." What is secretly communicated to the child is, "You are a failure, and you need me to protect and direct you in life," thereby strengthening the co-dependency.

Through subconscious reinforcement, the child starts performing for his or her parent's approval. He or she so desperately wants to meet his or her parents' expectations and do right (this is why they have a strong conscience of right from wrong). The problem is the parent doesn't want to let go of the control they have over their child. So, they hold onto their codependent belief that my child just won't make it in this world without me. To reinforce this belief, they begin criticizing the child when they do something wrong. The underlying message the child receives from his mom or dad is that love is conditional. If they do not perform to the perfect standards their parents have set for them, they will not feel or be loved.

If they do not become aware of the stronghold that binds them, their critical spirit will lead to a codependent conditional loving relationship with their children, thus passing the stronghold to their children. This, my friend, is exactly where Satan wants them.

How to Recognize a Beaver:

Everything they own is clean, organized, and/or well arranged. Just look in their closet and you'll see all their clothes neatly organized and color coordinated. Their desk will be neat and orderly. Their car (if they own one), spotless inside and out.

They get frustrated when leaving things undone. They hate leaving for school without make-up on, brushing their teeth, making their bed, etc. Everything must be in its place. This can cause them to be late.

They are highly critical of themselves and others.

They can be moody. When complimented, they feel good. When criticized, they feel bad.

They have performance anxiety.

They ask, "How?" How do I ... How do you ...

They often say, "I don't understand why you would want to be my friend," especially after they may have let you down.

The Golden Retriever

One of the most docile pets on this earth is a Golden Retriever. They are so precious as puppies. What I find most amazing about these creatures is their sincerity of heart, and their incredible sense of devotion and loyalty to their master. They also make the worst guard dogs because they rarely bark at newcomers. Instead, they wag their tail and act cute hoping the newcomer will notice them. Likewise, they rarely get into trouble; and when they do, they seem so dejected and miserable. Aristotle, Plato, C.S. Lewis, Saran Kierkegaard, Hemingway, Arnold Sweitzer, Mahatma Gandhi, Martin Luther King, Will Rogers, and Charlie Brown are but a few of the famous Golden Retrievers that have walked this earth. Biblical Golden Retrievers include Martha's sister Mary, Timothy, and Barnabas. The predominant Golden Retriever makes up just ten percent of the students that go to your school.

The Golden Retriever's Strengths:

No one has a bad thing to say about a true Golden Retriever. They are the most wonderful friends you can have. If you want to feel loved, approved of, and accepted, build your friendships around a bunch of Golden Retrievers.

More than any other personality, they have a deep longing to know where they "fit in" to their family, their school, the teams they play on, their youth group, and in the world as a whole. They hunger for the sentimental answers of "Who am I? Why am I here? and How do I become the person I really am?" They value intimacy in relationships and often are described as "deep" in relating to others. Often, they will look for ways to express themselves through art, theatre, music, and/or writing. They love to use their literary skills to persuade others and to promote change in society. Hollywood is full of Golden Retrievers.

Golden Retrievers have a tremendous drive for authenticity. What you see is what you get. They hate hypocrites and stay away from people who are fake. They are humble and vulnerable, often crying on a whim, not only for themselves, but for others. They are the ones who cry at sentimental holiday commercials. Likewise, they love to laugh with people and have an appreciation for good humor. Often their humor is described as dry and witty.

Like no other, they search for meaning in their life and find their significance through serving society. They make great leaders although they tend to shy from such positions. Whereas the lion tends to motivate through fear, the Golden Retriever tends to motivate through love and inspiration. They have the gift of persuasion. Rarely do they push their ideas on others.

They are supportive of their friends and family. More than any other personality type, the dominant Golden Retriever has a genuine sincerity for others and live for true relationships in their life. They are highly skilled with people. Simply put, they love people. They see everyone as a gift. They see potential and possibility in everyone and believe in society's throwaways. They have no problem overlooking another's weaknesses. Often, they carry an incredible sense of burden for those who are hurting and have a desire to rescue and rebuild lives. They sacrifice to support those in need. As a friend, they are soft, kind, compassionate, loyal, sincere, authentic, inspirational, humble, sympathetic, gentle, easy going, warm, fun, accepting, nurturing, patient, punctual, and a good listener.

Of all people, they are the most loved because they are sensitive. They are the nerve endings of relationships always in touch with their feelings and the feelings of those around them.

By nature, they are diplomatic and nonabrasive when crisis arises, always looking for ways to make peace within their circle of friends. They have a deep understanding of group dynamics and are incredibly perceptive to the different levels of communication going on within their circle of friends. They can bring people of different backgrounds together to accept one another's ways of being. Because of this usually they become the person everyone goes to when they have a problem. As a matter of fact, they almost always gravitate to counseling, psychology, nursing, ministry, and other serving vocations as a career.

The Golden Retriever is sentimental. Everything in their life has meaning. They collect everything and never throw anything away. Why? Because they love to reminisce about times gone by. It takes them forever to clean up their room because they tend to get caught up in their stuff.

Finally, unlike the otter, Golden Retrievers hold to the promises they make. They are committed to their friends and family for life. They will work themselves into exhaustion to uphold their commitments. Rarely do you see a Golden Retriever break a promise without feeling bad.

The Golden Retriever's Weaknesses:

No other personality deals with self-confidence issues the way a Golden Retriever does. They tend to underestimate their value and ability. They are so quick to point out their imperfections often admitting they will try harder to get it right next time. Those who hang out with Golden Retrievers will feel frustrated at times because they can see so much raw potential and ability in them that is never tapped (1 Timothy 4:14). They will often underestimate their contribution to others and feel they should have done more.

More so than the beaver, they struggle with strong feelings of inadequacy and negative self-talk which stops them from starting and/or completing projects. This gives them the appearance of laziness and procrastination. They love to be entertained. They long for a life that is happy, pleasant, and peace filled. They enjoy activities that are non-competitive and relaxing. Rarely do they establish goals and/or plan anything out of fear they will fail anyway. Much like the otter, the classic Golden Retriever will find they have great ideas, false starts, and unfinished projects. They are known to have huge dreams yet lack the confidence to carry them out.

They often become spectators, enjoying the sidelines of life, however, they truly desire to get into the game yet don't have the confidence to do so. No one disqualifies himself from having what he wants quicker than the Golden Retriever. Likewise, when participating, they are extremely careful not to upset others. This makes them appear timid and shy when competing. On rare occasions, when those they love are being threatened, they can become aggressive.

Golden Retrievers hate conflict and will do whatever they can to avoid it. They will withdraw, hide, compromise, or even say "yes" when they really want to say "no." They are also the people pleasers of the world often allowing their peers to lead them. As a matter of fact, every lion probably has a handful of Golden Retrievers following him or her around. This sets them up to look like the peacekeeper in their circle of friends and is also the reason why so many Golden Retrievers are so cleverly diplomatic. Avoidance of conflict causes them to compromise their beliefs and drift with society. Likewise, because they see potential and possibility in those society has otherwise written off, they tend to be tolerant of others' sin, and err on the side of grace (1 Timothy 1:4, 4:6-7). Peacekeeping and a strong desire to please others often leaves them overwhelmed and overworked. This makes them appear tired all the time.

Finally, they rarely fight for attention often drawing themselves into isolation. Because of their poor self-image, they tend to be overly conscientious of their appearance. Often, they humbly accept they cannot change their image and accept themselves as a failure. This hopelessness reinforces their negative self-talk and sets them up to become apathetic and lazy. They may go in and out of obesity, eating disorders, and depression. Too much Golden Retriever can possibly lead to suicide.

The Underlying Stronghold of False Belief That Binds:

What sits at the bottom of someone who has too much Golden Retriever is the false belief: **I am who I am. I cannot change. I am hopeless.** More than anything **Golden Retrievers fear abandonment**. It is for this reason they strive to "fit in." They just want to know someone approves of them for who they are. Their idol, the pagan god they serve in this world, is **"being comfortable."** They look for comfort to ease their sense of hopelessness; food, movies, books, computers, drugs, whatever it takes. Eating disorders become habit forming especially the eating disorder bulimia. They turn to bingeing for comfort, then struggle with obesity. Likewise, they strive for significance through relationships. After all, "If I have friends who like me, then I'm not a loser."

Golden Retrievers are raised in a home where they may have been victimized by circumstances in their life. Often, they have been betrayed or abandoned by their parents at an early age. This leaves them with the sense, "Something's wrong with me." Abandonment takes on many forms. Some may be placed for adoption, others may be the middle or "lost child" in the family dynamics, and still others may be raised in a household where his or her parents are emotionally unavailable to nurture and love them.

Often, they use the strategy of self-pity to draw concern and affection from those who care. Unfortunately, this victimization backfires on them as friends and family begin feeling manipulated by their self-pity. This, in turn, reinforces the belief, "I am who I am. I cannot change. I am hopeless," and throws them further into despair and depression. Depending upon the degree of abandonment they've experienced as a child, if they do not become aware of the stronghold that binds them, their desire to manipulate others into caring for them can lead to being emotionally unavailable to nurture and love their spouse and children thus passing on the cycle of sin to their children. This, my friend, is exactly where Satan wants them.

How to Recognize a Golden Retriever:

Quiet. Have you ever heard a Golden Retriever bark when someone comes to the door?

Sincere. Rarely do you hear sarcasm come out of their mouth.

Simple. They don't try to impress because they don't think anyone will notice.

They follow. Rarely do they take a leadership role.

Creative. They have incredible creative minds. They love to make things that are unique or novel. This could be in the form of music, drawing, inventing.

They think deep and enjoy deep sentimental conversation.

They can fall prey to depression and self-pity.

What's Your Dominant Personality?

It is important to understand, that each of us has a bit of all four personalities built into our being, however, one or two dominate who we are. Golden Retrievers do have some lion in them, and beavers have some playful otter in them. Sometimes this makes it a bit more difficult to figure out which is dominant.

Have you been able to identify your dominant personality? Who would you say you are? What false beliefs cause you to be this type of person? How about your mom, dad, sisters and brothers? What type of personality do they have? Sometimes it is easier to start with who you are not and eliminate those that don't fit. Often a lion has little Golden Retriever, and a beaver has little otter in them because they are opposites of each other.

One last point. It is important to realize; you can possess the strengths of a personality without the weaknesses. Remember, weaknesses are driven by the stronghold of false belief deep within our subconscious. Likewise, it is important to understand that although we all tend to migrate toward one or two personality types, with intent, we can possess the characteristics of all four. This is what Doctors. Smalley and Trent call maturing. The ability of the Golden Retriever to step up and lead or the Lion to step down and follow however uncomfortable it may feel is a true sign of maturity. God wants us to grow as people as well as Christians and often it requires us to be vulnerable and do things we may find uncomfortable.

This has been a long chapter and I thank you for hanging in there and reading it. It was designed to equip you with a spiritual power called discernment. Discernment is the beginning of wisdom (Hebrews 5:14). When God brings you into another's life, He is calling you to discern who this person is and how you can selflessly serve them the way Christ would. Figuring out or discerning their personality is the first step to having a meaningful relationship with them. And with the law of reaping and sowing, as you sow into these relationships, you will reap an ever-growing circle of friends at your school. The larger your circle of friends become, the more influence you have. And influence is what ultimately brings change. **This is the Divine Secret—living selflessly for another to serve God.**

Now it is time to get with your mentor to discuss this chapter and possibly do another challenge. This should be a fun one as you talk about who you are and who your mentor is. May the Force be with you and your mentor.

QUOTABLES:

Arthur Katz in his book *The Spirit of Truth*:

"Truth is threatening to us. We live in fear of truth and so structure our marriages and relationships in churches to insulate and protect us from it. Church, family, and fellowship have evolved into elaborate systems for avoiding conflict and exposure and for skirting issues. The very architecture of most churches and families, and our whole way of conducting services is perfectly suited to keeping any real involvement in the daily reality of each other's lives to an absolute minimum. Then in our varying degrees of insulation, effectively cut off from any intimate contact with God or man, we cry out in desperation for love. The gnawing hunger in our heart persists. We begin by insulating ourselves from the truth in order to protect ourselves, but we end up by insulating ourselves from love. Shielding ourselves from truth does not protect love, it suffocates it. The only thing preserved by being sheltered from truth, call it whatever else you will, is a lie. The most overlooked and neglected remedy for lovelessness is a large dose of truthfulness."

NOTABLES:

I have developed an app that you can download that will help you figure out a person's personality. Go to www.theG2C.com to download.

.

Notes:

Stronghold: I must meet certain standards
            to feel loved or accepted
Idol: Looking Good
Personality: Lion
Fear: Failure

Stronghold: I must be approved of by certain
            people in my life to feel loved or accepted.
Idol: Feeling Good
Personality: Otter
Fear: Rejection

Stronghold: If I fail, I don't deserve to be
            loved or accepted and should be punished.
Idol: Being Right
Personality: Beaver
Fear: Punishment

Stronghold: I am who I am. I cannot change.
            I am hopeless.
Idol: Being Comfortable
Personality: Golden Retriever
Fear: Abandonment

4

THE RABBIT HOLE

Have you ever stood and stared at it? Its beauty. Its genius. Billions of people just living out their lives, oblivious.

The Matrix, 1999; Warner Brothers

What is your life? You are a mist that appears for a little while then vanishes.

James 4:14 NIV

If you take the blue pill, the story ends; you wake up in your bed and believe what you want to believe. Take the red pill, you stay in wonderland, and I show you how deep the rabbit hole goes.

The Matrix, 1999; Warner Brothers

Have you ever wondered how Satan draws a person away from God? I've always argued if you were to taste God's love just once, you'd never walk away from Him. But somehow Satan gets Christians to walk away from the deepest love and acceptance they will ever feel. How? One way, and I venture to guess, the most effective, is to pre-occupy a person so that he or she has no time left to be with their heavenly Father.

In his book, *Tipping Point* by Malcolm Gladwell, he writes of a social study done by two Princeton University psychologists John Darley and Daniel Batson. The object of the study was to reenact the story of the Good Samaritan with a bit of a twist (Luke 10:30–37). They wanted to see if being busy had any effect on a servant's heart.

The study was simple yet beautifully scripted. Between two campus buildings of the Princeton Theological Seminary school was a courtyard that students had to walk through to get from one building to the other. Darley and Batson met with a handful of seminary students asking them to prepare a short talk on a Biblical theme. Some were asked to speak on the relevance of clergy to the religious vocation. Others were asked to speak on the parable of the Good Samaritan.

After they were given ample time to prepare their talk, Batson and Darley would call the student in and say, "Oh you're late. They were expecting you a few minutes ago, we better get moving." They were then directed to head over to the conference room across the courtyard. Office staff really sold the students on the urgency of the matter as faculty with busy schedules were waiting.

In the courtyard lay a man face down, obviously beaten, eyes closed, and groaning. The question these psychology professors wanted to answer was: would a man who has made a choice to devote his life to God and helping others have time to do God's work if he was busy and under stress? The answer: 90% of the students stepped over the beaten man to *not be late* to do a task. Incredulously, only 10% of the students stopped. Wow! These were young men with a heart to serve. But the study wasn't done.

Darley and Batson then decided to take the stress away to see if the students would respond differently. In this scenario, everything remained the same except instead of a bunch of faculty nervously waiting for a student to give his presentation, the student was informed that a meeting would take place "in a few minutes." They then suggested he get over there early to prepare.

Once again, the student encountered the bruised and obviously beaten man, but this time without the sense of urgency. The results were staggering. 63% of the students stopped to help. In his conclusion, Gladwell writes, "What this study is suggesting, in other words, is that the convictions of your heart, and the actual contents of your thoughts, are less important in the end in guiding your actions than the immediate context of your behavior. The words of 'Oh, you're late' have the effect of turning someone who was ordinarily compassionate into someone who was indifferent to suffering; of turning someone in that particular moment into a different person."

Is your life busy? Do you already have an intense schedule? Are you striving to have a better life by spending countless hours studying, on the practice field, or _____ (fill in the blank)? If so, you may be falling prey to one of Satan's biggest strategies.

The 48-Hour Work Week

Ninety miles an hour going fast as I can
Trying to push a little harder, trying to get the upper hand
So much to do in so little time, it's a crazy life.

Jonny Diaz, *Breathe*

The lives of Americans are becoming busier and busier by the day. According to the National Labor Board, the number of working hours has steadily increased over time. In 1970, the average work week for an American was 35 hours, and bills and mortgages could be paid with a single income. By 2012, this number had increased to 46.7 hours per week with bills and mortgages requiring a dual income. Worse yet, income levels have declined by 5% since the 9/11 attacks on the World Trade Center in New York. This coupled with the fact that we live in an age when parents don't feel safe to allow their children out of their sight, has left them with little time as they run their children from one organized activity to the next.

It is the classic case of "I have to work more because I make less" scenario. Workaholism is no longer the exception in our society, it is the norm. And to further muddy the waters, if one were to have the gall to only work 40 hours a week and only have one parent working, one would have to be willing to have a lot less and deal with peers who don't quite understand what they are doing. This would mean no financial planning, no retirement, no healthcare, no mortgage, etc.

Is the devil behind all this? You better believe he is. So many young Christians are like those young men in the seminary study. Life has taken on an urgency like no other, and the result is no time to serve the Lord. What will the future hold for Americans? Are we going to get busier? By the time you enter the workforce what do you think the average work week will be? 48 hours? That's a whole extra day a week! That means you'd be working Monday through Saturday to meet the demands of your job.

I believe this is exactly what is going to happen. America is caught up in an obese government that continues to gain weight. So many industries are now regulated or controlled by the government. With these regulations come more paperwork and steps to the working process. This usually results in more time as the documentation must be filled out. It also means government officials can terminate your business if you don't follow their time-consuming regulations. The amount of paperwork your doctor generates in one day is absolutely mind blowing. One thing is certain, our government loves to govern so it's not going away. Simply put, if the government didn't require so much time-consuming paperwork, we all would be less inclined to work so many hours.

So, what does all this talk have to do with you, a teenager in high school? Simple—you are going to have to make a choice; do I succumb to the devil's scheme and busy my life, or do I purpose my life to serve God? According to the Bible, you cannot serve two masters; you cannot serve both God and materialism (Matthew 6:19-24). As you leave college and enter the work force, you will be faced with a decision. "Do I live the American dream and go deeply into debt to have the degree, the house, the car, and lifestyle I've always dreamed of?" or "Do I live to stay out of debt, work less and have more free time to love on and serve others?"

Gee, this sounds so eerily familiar to what young Thomas Anderson faced in *The Matrix*. Do I take the blue pill and wake up as if nothing happened, or do I take the red pill and see how deep the rabbit hole goes? *The Matrix* isn't as farfetched as it appears to be.

Defeating Satan: Easier Said Than Done

Defeating Satan requires you to make a choice to not serve yourself, but serve others, and in that choice, have all the love and contentment you could ever imagine. There is a story that has been used to illustrate this point in many different versions. The story kind of goes like this:

There was a young stockbroker from Wall Street who, because of the stress of his job, started having health issues. His doctor told him he was overworked and overstressed and needed to take a vacation. He decided to travel to a small Mexican fishing village off the coast of Baja where there was no internet or cell signal. Every morning he would wake up and go down to the beach and watch the waves, and every morning he noticed a local villager fishing off the coast. The man would catch enough fish for his family and some more to be sold at the village market.

After a few days, and with his broken Spanish, this young stock broker approached the local fisherman. "I noticed you fishing every morning. How are the fish?"

"Oh, they are good, señor," he answered with surprisingly good English.

The young man then asked, "I noticed you fish only until 7 a.m. Why not stay out and catch more?"

"Well, señor, I only catch enough fish for my family and then some to take to the market. That is all I need."

"Then what do you do with the rest of your day?" the young man asked.

"I go home to help my wife with the chores, eat lunch, take a siesta, then in the evening, my wife and I head to the village where I get with my comrades to drink wine and sing songs," the fisherman responded.

The young man pressed in. "You know, you could have so much more if you got a loan, bought a bigger boat, and fished longer."

"And why would I want do this?" asked the fisherman.

"Well, if you had a bigger boat you could catch more fish to sell at the market. More fish would mean more money. With the money, you could buy more boats to build your business. Then, you could employ your 'comrades' to work with you and eventually erect a cannery here in the village and employ the people to work in the cannery."

"And why would I want to do this, señor?" asked the fisherman once again.

"Well, then you could take your business to the stock market where people could invest in your dream," the young man retorted.

Still puzzled the fisherman asked yet once again, "And why would I want to do this, señor?"

"Well, with more money, you could invest in more boats. More boats equal more fish, which equals more canneries. Then you would have an empire of canneries up and down this coast, and with it more money than you would know what to do with," exclaimed the young man with excitement!

"And if I did all this, then what?" asked the fisherman.

"Then you could sleep in, go to the market in the morning, come home to help your wife with the chores, eat lunch, take a siesta and meet up with your comrades to drink wine and sing songs in the village square each evening," replied the young stockbroker.

At some point, you have to ask yourself, "Why am I doing this?" Is it for selfish ambition, fame, or recognition? Another important question to ask is, "Who or what am I doing this for?" Listen to your answers as they will tell you a lot about your future. Pray to your Heavenly Father asking Him to reveal your true motives in life. If your motives are for Him, great. If not, you may be falling right into Satan's trap. Like Jesus said, you will learn to serve one and hate the other. The choice is yours and there is no better time than today to decide who or what you want to serve.

Tapping into God's Supernatural Powers

The first step to tapping into God's supernatural powers is to un-busy your life. The next step is to take all that time you've saved and use it to influence your friends. One of the biggest ways you can influence your friends is to speak truth into their lives. When you speak the truth, you effectively unbind the stronghold Satan has on them. Remember, Satan tailors lies to fit certain personalities. By speaking against these lies, you effectively free your friend up to be who God created them to be (John 8:32). In the remainder of this chapter, we are going to take a hard look at how Jesus did this to see how we can do the same.

How to Make a Difference in a Lion's World

This is no easy task. Lions are extremely strong, confident people that don't put a lot of weight on relationships. If strong in their personality and a bit immature, they tend to not want to listen to advice. To gain some insight on how to approach a lion, let's look at how Jesus worked with lions in a couple of passages in the Bible.

In Mathew 23, we see Jesus taking on the Pharisees who boasted of being the godliest of all people. Jesus, knowing the pride and arrogance of their hearts, spoke to them in front of the people. What he said was powerful and a lesson for us all to learn. Starting at verse 12 and continuing to verse 36, this is what He said,

> Whoever exalts himself shall be humbled; and whoever humbles himself shall be exalted.

Eight Woes

"But woe to you, scribes and Pharisees, hypocrites, because you shut off the kingdom of heaven from people; for you do not enter in yourselves, nor do you allow those who are entering to go in. Woe to you, scribes and Pharisees, hypocrites, because you devour widows' houses, and for a pretense you make long prayers; therefore, you will receive greater condemnation.

"Woe to you, scribes and Pharisees, hypocrites, because you travel around on sea and land to make one proselyte; and when he becomes one, you make him twice as much a son of hell as yourselves.

"Woe to you, blind guides, who say, 'Whoever swears by the temple, *that* is nothing; but whoever swears by the gold of the temple is obligated.' You fools and blind men! Which is more important, the gold or the temple that sanctified the gold? And, 'Whoever swears by the altar, *that* is nothing, but whoever swears by the offering on it, he is obligated.' You blind men, which is more important, the offering, or the altar that sanctifies the offering? Therefore, whoever swears by the altar, swears *both* by the altar and by everything on it. And whoever swears by the temple, swears *both* by the temple and by Him who dwells within it. And whoever swears by heaven, swears *both* by the throne of God and by Him who sits upon it.

"Woe to you, scribes and Pharisees, hypocrites! For you tithe mint and dill and cummin and have neglected the weightier provisions of the law: justice and mercy and faithfulness; but these are the things you should have done without neglecting the others. You blind guides, who strain out a gnat and swallow a camel!

"Woe to you, scribes and Pharisees, hypocrites! For you clean the outside of the cup and of the dish, but inside they are full of robbery and self-indulgence. You blind Pharisee, first clean the inside of the cup and of the dish, so that the outside of it may become clean also.

"Woe to you, scribes and Pharisees, hypocrites! For you are like whitewashed tombs which on the outside appear beautiful, but inside they are full of dead men's bones and all uncleanness. So you, too, outwardly appear righteous to men, but inwardly you are full of hypocrisy and lawlessness.

"Woe to you, scribes and Pharisees, hypocrites! For you build the tombs of the prophets and adorn the monuments of the righteous, and say, 'If we had been *living* in the days of our fathers, we would not have been partners with them in *shedding* the blood of the prophets.' So you testify against yourselves, that you are sons of those who murdered the prophets. Fill up, then, the measure *of the guilt* of your fathers. You serpents, you brood of vipers, how will you escape the sentence of hell?

"Therefore, behold, I am sending you prophets and wise men and scribes; some of them you will kill and crucify, and some of them you will scourge in your synagogues, and persecute from city to city, so that upon you may fall *the guilt of* all the righteous blood shed on earth, from the blood of righteous Abel to the blood of Zechariah, the son of Berechiah, whom you murdered between the temple and the altar. Truly I say to you, all these things will come upon this generation.

Matthew 23:12-36

As you can see, Jesus is not being tender, understanding, or supportive. Instead, He is being direct, contentious, and convincing. He is speaking to them in a language they understand. If anything is going to wake these guys up, it is this no-nonsense approach. Believe it or not, Jesus is loving the Pharisees He is speaking to in this passage. He is wanting them to see the hypocrisy they are living in, in hopes they will "wake up" and change.

Yes, his approach is direct, but with logic. Notice after He says, "Woe to you," he follows with a question. Although they follow a logical path, these questions aren't open-ended. The questions are intended to break through the stronghold. He is truly trying to turn the hearts of these men back to him. Simply put, He has confronted them in their evil ways and challenged them to change.

If we see a lion friend who professes to be Christian, yet takes advantage of his friends for personal gain, what are we left to do, but confront? It's the two-facedness that reveals the stronghold. The stronghold is what is holding this person back. God places us in a position to speak into this person's heart in love. Being anything but direct would in fact not work with a lion and they are matter of fact and to the point. In other words, trying to be tender to a lion all in the guise of "Love" just won't work.

Now let's look at a passage where Jesus spoke one on one to a lion with a little more humility. What we are about to see is the same direct no nonsense approach, but with dialog. I take you to the third chapter of John when Jesus has the conversation of being "born again" with Nicodemus, a Pharisee.

Now there was a man of the Pharisees named Nicodemus, a ruler of the Jews; this man came to Jesus by night and said to him, "Rabbi, we know that you have come from God, as a teacher; for no one can do these signs that You do unless God is with him." [Nicodemus is investigating this on his own time and out of the eye of his peers because he knows he can't clearly assess Jesus under the criticism of his peers.] Jesus answered and said to him, "Truly, truly, I say to you, unless one is 'born' again he cannot see the kingdom of God." Nicodemus said to him, "How can a man be born when he is old? He cannot enter a second time into his mother's womb and be born, can he?" [Much like an attorney in the courtroom, Nicodemus is challenging Jesus with a question that requires Jesus to prove his accusation. This is how lions operate.] Jesus answered, "Truly, truly, I say to you, unless one is born of water and the Spirit, he cannot enter the kingdom of God. That which is born of the flesh is flesh, and that which is born of the Spirit is spirit. Do not marvel that I said to you, 'You must be born again.' The wind blows where it wishes, and you hear its sound, but you do not know where it comes from or where it goes. So it is with everyone who is born of the Spirit." [Jesus is now challenging Nicodemus to understand the universe in a way never presented to him before. This is a challenge for Nicodemus to go to a place in his mind he has never gone.]

Nicodemus said to him, "How can these things be?" Jesus answered and said to him, "Are you the teacher of Israel and do not understand these things? Truly, truly, I say to you, we speak of what we know, and testify of what we have seen, but you do not accept our testimony. If I told you earthly things and you do not believe, how will you believe heavenly things?" [Jesus continues to reinforce his argument with direct questions, "Is it possible you do not know all there is to know about the universe?] No one has ascended into heaven, but He who descended from heaven; the Son of Man. As Moses lifted up the serpent in the wilderness, even so must the Son of Man be lifted up; so that whoever believes in him will have eternal life."

For God So Loved the World

"For God so loved the world, that he gave his only begotten Son, that whoever believes in him shall not perish but have eternal life. For God did not send the Son into the world to judge the world, but that the world might be saved through him. He who believes in him is not judged; he who does not believe has been judged already, because he has not believed in the name of the only begotten Son of God. And this is the judgment, that the light has come into the world, and men loved the darkness rather than the Light, for their deeds were evil. For everyone who does evil hates the Light, and does not come to the Light for fear that his deeds will be exposed. But he who practices the truth comes to the Light, so that his deeds may be manifest as having been wrought in God."

John 3:1-21

Although Nicodemus shows the tendency of a lion to **look good**, he is willing to entertain discussion outside of his comfort zone. This is a sign of maturity. He is willing to weigh the facts and dialog with another, before making a decision. In this instance, Jesus is as direct as he was when speaking to the Pharisees in Mathew Chapter 23. He is asking Nicodemus to question his own understanding and conclude what is real.

How to Speak into the Heart of a Lion

The best way to speak into a lion's heart is to be direct and to the point. Provided you are a good friend, if you see them struggling, let them know why. Lions have a lot of common sense. If you can back up what you are saying with facts, they tend to listen. As much as you can speak to the stronghold and not the weakness. Remember, the stronghold is "I must meet certain standards to feel loved," and "looking good" is the idol they serve. Remember, their stronghold is deeply rooted in their subconscious, so they may not understand their desire to achieve and be better than everyone else.

A simple question could be all it takes: "Why do you think you need to _____ (achievement, i.e., win all the time, get an A on your test, be the class president, etc.) to feel good about yourself?"

If you can draw the stronghold up from their subconscious, the lion will begin to understand himself or herself in a way that allows healing. Sometimes, however, in your best effort to make a difference, your good friend may feel attacked, and he or she will roar to defend their position. The discussion can get contentious. Be ready and stick to the facts. It's hard to argue against what is true. It's natural for us all to defend what isn't working in our lives. You may walk away thinking you got nowhere. Don't be fooled, lions are incredibly smart people. If you present to them you care about them and that they are hurting themselves by being this way, they will listen.

How to Make a Difference in an Otter's World

There was no one who better exemplified how to bring down the strongholds of unbelief than Jesus. He is the example we all should take note from. How did Jesus speak to an otter? How did he handle a playful otter's fear of rejection and the need to "feel good"? Peter was undoubtedly an otter. He had a strong desire to be the center of attention. "Feeling good," was the pagan god he served. All we have to do is look at how Jesus spoke to and interacted with Peter to understand how to work with an otter.

In the 21st chapter of John, Jesus encounters Peter and the disciples after he had been crucified. If you remember the story, Peter had denied Jesus three times the night before he hung on the cross for our sins. Peter has felt shame ever since, He knew he was wrong, and it hurt deeply. So, let's pick up the story in John 21.

After this, Jesus appeared again to the disciples, this time at the Tiberias Sea (the Sea of Galilee). This is how he did it: Simon Peter, Thomas (nicknamed "Twin"), Nathanael from Cana in Galilee, the brothers Zebedee, and two other disciples were together. Simon Peter announced, "I'm going fishing."

The rest of them replied, "We're going with you." They went out and got in the boat. They caught nothing that night. When the sun came up, Jesus was standing on the beach, but they didn't recognize him.

Jesus spoke to them: "Good morning! Did you catch anything for breakfast?"

They answered, "No."

He said, "Throw the net off the right side of the boat and see what happens."

They did what he said. All of a sudden there were so many fish in it, they weren't strong enough to pull it in.

Then the disciple Jesus loved said to Peter, "It's the Master!"

When Simon Peter realized that it was the Master, he threw on some clothes, for he was stripped for work, and dove into the sea. The other disciples came in by boat for they weren't far from land, a hundred yards or so, pulling along the net full of fish. When they got out of the boat, they saw a fire laid, with fish and bread cooking on it.

Jesus said, "Bring some of the fish you've just caught." Simon Peter joined them and pulled the net to shore—153 big fish! And even with all those fish, the net didn't rip.

Jesus said, "Breakfast is ready." Not one of the disciples dared ask, "Who are you?" They knew it was the Master.

Jesus then took the bread and gave it to them. He did the same with the fish. This was now the third time Jesus had shown himself alive to the disciples since being raised from the dead."

Do You Love Me?

After breakfast, Jesus said to Simon Peter, "Simon, son of John, do you love me more than these?"

"Yes, Master, you know I love you."

Jesus said, "Feed my lambs."

He then asked a second time, "Simon, son of John, do you love me?"

"Yes, Master, you know I love you."

Jesus said, "Shepherd my sheep."

Then he said it a third time: "Simon, son of John, do you love me?"

Peter was upset that he asked for the third time, "Do you love me?" so he answered, "Master, you know everything there is to know. You've got to know that I love you."

Jesus said, "Feed my sheep. I'm telling you the very truth now: When you were young you dressed yourself and went wherever you wished, but when you get old you'll have to stretch out your hands while someone else dresses you and takes you where you don't want to go." He said this to hint at the kind of death by which Peter would glorify God. And then he commanded, "Follow me."

John 21:1-19 (MSG)

So here we have Jesus (God) speaking into the heart of a wounded otter, Peter. How did Jesus speak to Peter? If you answered directly, then you would be right. When Jesus commissioned Peter to "Lead my people," what was his tone? If you said tender, you'd be right. Remember, what sits at the heart of an otter is a strong fear of rejection, and Peter is no different. He feared deeply Jesus had rejected him since he denied Jesus that night. Have you ever been in a place where you know you wronged someone, then saw them again among friends? Did it feel kind of weird, like you knew you needed to have a conversation with them, but there really wasn't an opportunity? I imagine this was where Peter was at when Jesus appeared to the disciples in the upper room after He rose again. It just wasn't the right time to clear things up.

So, Jesus being Jesus makes the effort to let Peter know he doesn't reject Him. Instead, He loves him despite Peter's faults and He wants Peter to understand how much He believes in Peter's ability to lead his people.

This is why he was becoming frustrated with Jesus asking the same question over and over again. In Peter's mind, he knows he loves Jesus and he is starting to wonder what Jesus is doing, so he becomes emphatic in his answer.

Jesus, on the other hand is working to slow down Peter's thought process. He wants Peter to understand the brevity of what He is asking, "Do...you...love...me?"

Like all strong otters, Jesus knows Peter's desire is to be admired and accepted by others including Jesus himself. So, staring directly into his eyes, he asks the question. The question that Peter needed to answer for healing to take place in his heart, "Do you love me?" Each time it forces Peter to listen to what Jesus is saying. And with each answer, He begins to understand the challenge Jesus is placing before him.

After much prayer and consideration, I believe this is what Peter heard when he really started to understand the question Jesus was asking. Three times Jesus asks the question, and three times Peter feels the call, the challenge to lead. This is no simple undertaking. The weight of his decision is huge. Jesus needs no flippant answer from an otter here. He needs an answer that will change the world. And Peter, after three questions, finally gets the weight of what Jesus is asking. And when Peter gives his final answer "Yes," I can only imagine it was loud, resolute, and with excitement!

In this brief study on how Jesus treated an otter, we see Him having to get beyond the empty promise, "Yea, sure Jesus, I'll do it." Instead, Jesus wants this otter to feel the weight of this incredible responsibility.

If I were Jesus, there is no way I'm calling on a guy who betrayed me to lead my cause. Would you? The natural reaction is to go to the guy who wronged you and demand an apology in front of all your friends. But this would drive the shame even deeper into the psyche of this otter, and because he is all about "feeling good," our friendship would pretty much be over. He would walk away thinking, *"I'll never hang with him again."*

If, on the other hand, you take the narrow path and defy logic like Jesus, your relationship will be restored. In the moment, Jesus is asking Peter to lead his people, he is admitting forgiveness of Peter's actions the night before he died. Otters are going to say things they don't mean all the time. It's our job as Christians to realize this and get these otters to stop and think about what they are saying. Interesting, isn't it? An otter fears rejection, strives to be accepted, says yes to everything which causes rejection and pain to those who care. This ultimately brings on the one thing they fear as their friends walk away shaking their head in disgust. Go figure.

How to Speak into the Heart of an Otter

Often, the dominant otter will listen to feedback if framed the right way. Like anyone else, you must first ask permission to be honest with them and you must be a close enough friend to have earned their trust. Let them know you aren't joking and it is important they get serious for a second. Although your words may be piercing, otters really want to know what you think of them. Likewise, they rarely see where they've wronged others because they have no sense of consequence for their actions. When they break their promises, it is vital you help them see the betrayal they are causing. Something like this really grabs their attention, "I have to be serious here for a minute and ask you a question that has been bugging me for some time." They will usually respond, "Okay, sure. What's up?" At which point you ask something like, "Why do you hide behind your humor?" They will usually respond, "What do you mean?" At which point, if you have their permission to speak to them in a heartfelt way, you say, "Well, I've noticed you stay light and funny with all of your friendships. I wonder if any of them really know who you are?"

How to Make a Difference in a Beaver's World

A passage worth unpacking that defines the character of a dominant beaver can be found in the book of John. After the death of Jesus, he appears to the disciples in the Upper Room. Thomas, however, wasn't there. When he returned, the disciples let him know Jesus was alive and had come to see them. Now Thomas had been around for some years and he knew when a man died, he wasn't coming back. Sure, he had witnessed Lazarus being raised from the dead by Jesus, but, the man who raised Lazarus was the man who died, so how could Jesus raise himself? To Thomas, this defied the laws of logic which can't happen.

Let's pick up the dialog Jesus has with Thomas in John Chapter 20.

> But Thomas, one of the twelve, called Didymus, was not with them when Jesus came. So the other disciples were saying to him, "We have seen the Lord!" But he said to them, "Unless I see in His hands the imprint of the nails, and put my finger into the place of the nails, and put my hand into His side, I will not believe."
>
> After eight days His disciples were again inside, and Thomas with them. Jesus came, the doors having been shut, and stood in their midst and said, "Peace *be* with you." Then He said to Thomas, "Reach here with your finger, and see My hands; and reach here your hand and put it into My side; and do not be unbelieving, but believing." Thomas answered and said to Him, "My Lord and my God!" Jesus said to him, "Because you have seen Me, have you believed? Blessed *are* they who did not see, and *yet* believed."
>
> John 20:24-29

As with most dominant beavers, they are not easily fooled. It is true, Thomas fled and did not see Christ crucified; however, he knew Christ had died because he was buried in a tomb. So, to hear his Christian brothers speak of Jesus appearing to them was a bit far-fetched. Beavers love science and more importantly laws. Laws are structured and can be followed. On the contrary, beavers can't stand exceptions. This is why most beavers love math and hate English. In math 2+2 is always 4, but in English, "I" comes before "E" except after "C" with exception to the rule. How many exceptions? Try 88. Almost

100 words do not follow this rule! If you are a true beaver, this is just one example of why you dread going to English class every day.

When Jesus confronted Thomas and his faith issues, He did it in a way that made sense to Thomas. "Here I am. Go ahead, conduct your experiment. Examine my hands. Touch my wounds. Place your hand into my side." And what was Thomas' conclusion? Jesus was God! Now let me ask you, will anything stand in the way of Thomas' faith now that he believes? Absolutely not. Once a beaver is convinced Jesus is Lord, his or her faith is unshakeable.

Now Jesus takes the opportunity to once again teach his disciples, "Because you have seen Me, have you believed? Blessed *are* they who did not see, and *yet* believed."

Was Jesus hard on Thomas for not believing much like he was with the Pharisees and Sadducees? No, this would have caused shame and guilt in Thomas' heart due to his critical spirit. No, Jesus knows Thomas' heart and the idol of "being right" that prevents him from "taking chances and being wrong," so Jesus tenderly allows Thomas to come to his own conclusion of what was evident.

As we see Jesus reaching into the heart of a beaver, we see a man (Jesus) who understands the stronghold of unbelief that Satan has on them—if I fail, I don't deserve to be loved and should be punished. He understands beavers live with no grace in their life; the stronghold won't allow it. So, Jesus gives them grace and in it, the stronghold is broken. They now can see that perfection in the eyes of peers (which is unattainable), doesn't match up to the freedom one has in Christ (which is attainable). Having to be perfect to be loved isn't freedom, it's bondage. Romans Chapter 8 makes it exceedingly clear, there is no condemnation, no judgement, no criticism of those who submit to Christ and remain in His grace. And with this comes freedom to express oneself without fear.

Remember when David danced before the Lord in his underwear (2 Samuel 6:12–23)? He had no concerns of what others thought. He was free. Michal, his wife, however, wasn't. She condemned David for his heart. As a beaver, she was embittered with a critical spirit. She was forever imprisoned and shameful of what she may look like before her friends instead of the freedom she could express before God. So, what does God do? He closes her womb not allowing her to have children. How unfortunate for David, a man living freely in God, and Michal, a woman so steeped in bondage to her stronghold that God saw it fitting to not allow her to raise David's children.

How to Speak into the Heart of a Beaver

The very thing beavers love, being critical, is the very thing that stops them in life. Helping a beaver take notice of this can be crucial to breaking their stronghold. Again, this type of conversation can only take place after you have walked the steps of intimacy with them and gotten to a place where you can share your heart. The conversation may look something like this. You: "Can I ask you a question?" Beaver: "What?" You: "Why are you so afraid of speaking in public?" Beaver: "I don't know. I guess I'm afraid of messing up. What does it matter?" You: "I don't know. I guess it's sad that you can't be you in front of all your friends without thinking they are judging you all the time. What would life look like if you didn't have to be so concerned about what your friends were thinking?" Beaver: "I don't know." You: "I just want you to know everyone on this planet makes mistakes every day. People get hurt by other people all the time. Walking through life being afraid to make a mistake is like living in a prison cell. I'm your friend and I'm not waiting for you to mess up, so I can call you on it. You are an incredible person and you have a voice. Don't be afraid to stand up and use it."

How to Make a Difference in A Golden Retriever's World

Once again, all we have to do is look to the model of Jesus to see how to interact with Golden Retrievers. I must admit, there aren't many passages to pick from as Golden Retrievers are quiet and therefore don't draw attention to themselves. There is a passage, however, where two sisters, one a Beaver, the other a Golden Retriever, have invited Jesus into their home for a warm meal. We find it in Luke Chapter 10.

Now as they were traveling along, He entered a village; and a woman named Martha welcomed Him into her home. She had a sister called Mary, who was seated at the Lord's feet, listening to His word. But Martha was distracted with all her preparations; and she came up *to Him* and said, "Lord, do You not care that my sister has left me to do all the serving alone? Then tell her to help me." But the Lord answered and said to her, "Martha, Martha, you are worried and bothered about so many things; but *only* one thing is necessary, for Mary has chosen the good part, which shall not be taken away from her."

Luke 10:38-42

What an incredible passage Jesus has left us with to understand how to interact with a Golden Retriever. Here are two sisters I would venture to guess well into their twenties and maybe even into their thirties. They lived together, or so it seems. We see one as being attentive and quiet, the other as frustrated and busy. What do you think is the personality type of Martha? If you said a Beaver, you'd be correct. This leaves Mary as our wonderful Golden Retriever so deeply, and I mean deeply, desiring to hear all that Jesus has to say.

Although it isn't written, I'm almost certain this isn't the first-time Martha, a dominant Beaver, was frustrated with her sister Mary, a dominant Golden Retriever, for not doing what seemed right. Martha, being hypercritical of her "preparations" as the Bible puts it, is scurrying around trying to get everything in its place so Jesus would give her the satisfaction of saying, "What a wonderful feast, Martha. I can tell you've worked hard on this meal and it was perfect." Jesus, however, knows He would be feeding into her stronghold of false belief if He did so. Instead He says, "you are worried and bothered about so many things; but *only* one thing is necessary." *The Message,* says it this way, "Martha, dear Martha, you're fussing far too much and getting yourself worked up over nothing." What is interesting to note is Martha was the one who invited Jesus to dinner, however, the Beaver in her wasn't ready for Him to come (I wonder if she'd ever be ready for Him to come?).

Mary, a Golden Retriever, could care less if everything was in its place. What matters most to her is bathing herself in her Lord's beauty, drinking in every word He has to offer. Remember her stronghold, **I am who I am. I cannot change. I am hopeless.** So, what does Jesus do? In perfect God fashion, He tears down both strongholds in one small yet direct sentence. To Martha, He is saying, "Martha, my dear Martha, your perfection is stopping you from having me right now," and to Mary He is saying, "Mary, my dear Mary, I care about you enough to stand for you. You matter to me, and you've chosen to do the right thing."

Jesus, in His defense of Mary, has lifted her confidence. It is a beautiful thing to see a Golden Retriever tear down their stronghold. They begin to realize the gift they are and begin to act on it.

There is a man in Ephesus who at the age of 40 decided to lead a church. He was being groomed by the apostle Paul to lead a small congregation in this newly formed religion called Christianity. His name was Timothy and he was a dominant Golden Retriever. How did

Paul lead this young pastor to greatness? If you read Timothy in the Bible, a common theme jumps out at you, "Timothy, I have faith in you. You can do this. You are a leader and God has qualified you to lead." He does not tell Timothy how to lead, he just let's Timothy know he has what it takes to lead. Paul, a mature Lion, finds leading as natural as breathing. He sees Timothy's potential as a leader, yet sees Timothy holding back out of fear he doesn't have what it takes. Instead of getting frustrated and impatient with Timothy (which is what a less mature Lion would do) Paul goes right into the need. He sees how God has groomed Timothy for such a time as this. He wants Timothy to grow and become the leader God has called him to be yet sees the stronghold that binds him. So, he douses him with compliments and encouragement.

How to Speak into the Heart of a Golden Retriever

Continually come alongside of them to help them appreciate the pricelessness of their individuality.

Encourage them to fulfill the promises they make to themselves and finish the projects they begin. (1 Timothy 4:14; 2 Timothy 2:15)

Encourage them to be strong as Paul did with Timothy. (2 Timothy 1:7; 2 Timothy 2:1)

Below their cool, timid personality, there is a tremendous amount of emotion boiling. Always be checking in with them. Make sure they are not falling into the sacrificial mode. Help them stand to the promises they make to themselves.

I started this chapter telling you about a social study where young seminary students literally walked over a beaten man because of scheduling issues. I then explained how Satan has taken this social study to the world by busying everyone's schedules. Next, we watched Jesus take down strongholds of the Lion, Beaver, Otter and Golden Retriever. It is awesome to think you can do the same. It just takes a little boldness and a lot of timing. Although none of your friends are dying on the side of the road like the Samaritan man, many are hiding emotional wounds inside their hearts. You've just learned how to speak into those hearts like Jesus to bring real healing. It just takes you to slow your life down just enough to reach out to them.

In this next chapter, we are going to look at another Samaritan story from the Bible called the woman at the well. We are going to see Jesus make time for this woman: wounded and outcast by society as He and His disciples go way out of their way to meet up with her. In this story, Jesus is once again going to teach us a few principles that will allow us to get close enough to our friends to talk to them in a real way. The biggest question is, will you un-busy your life to make the time? Now get with your mentor and discuss this chapter. He or she may have yet another challenge for you to do. May the Force be with you.

NOTABLES:

Want to know all 88 words that defy the "I" before "E" rule in the English language? Here they are:

Achieve, agreeing, albeit, Alzheimer's, atheism, beige, Beijing, being, caffeine, concierge, decide, deify, deign, deindustrialize, deisolate, deity, disagreeing, dreeing, dreidel, eight, either, Fahrenheit, feign, feisty, foreign, foreseeing, forfeit, freight, geitost, gesundheit, heifer, height, heinous, heir, heist, herein, inveigle, kaleidoscope, keister, lei, leisure, madeira, meiosis, neigh, neighbor, neither, obeisance, onomatopoeia, peine, protein, reign, reignite, reimburse, rein, reineer, reindustrialize, reinforce, reinstall, reinvest, reissue, safeish, scareabaeid, schlockmeister, science, seeing, seignorial, seine, seismic, seized sensei, sheik, skein, sleigh, sleight, sovereign, stein, surfeit, surveillance, their, theism, therein, veil, vein, weigh, weight, weir, weird, wherein, whereinto, xanthein, zootheism.

5

EARNING THE RIGHT TO BE HEARD

There's a hole in my soul and I can't fill it, I can't fill it.
There's a hole in my soul. Can You fill it? Can You fill it?

Bastille, *Flaws*

Even if your hands are shaking
And your faith is broken
Even as your eyes are closing
Do it with a heart wide open
Say what you need to say. Say what you need to say. Say
what you need to say.

John Mayer, *Say*

"I searched for a man among them who would build up the wall and stand in the gap before Me for the land, so that I would not destroy it; but I found no one. Thus, I have poured out My indignation on them; I have consumed them with the fire of My wrath; their way I have brought upon their heads," declares the Lord GOD.

Ezekiel 22:30-31

I'd like to tell you a story about a young man named Dennis who was raised on a farm back in the 1960s. Now God had given Dennis a gift that would change the world. As early as five years old, Dennis could listen to a song then play it on his parents' old piano. God had given him another gift. Dennis had a tender heart of compassion and could easily read the emotions of a room. If someone at his school were to accidentally slip and fall, instead of laughing with the rest of the kids, Dennis would identify with the embarrassment and shame of the person who fell.

Satan knew how powerful Dennis was and the plans God had for his life. So. he and his demons began to torment Dennis at a very young age. As Dennis entered middle school, his gift, the ability to play piano, grew. Unfortunately, on the world stage, pianists such as Liberace and Elton John were well known to be gay, so kids at school started to call him a faggot. Like most kids this age, Dennis' self-confidence was low, so he started to wonder if being a pianist automatically meant one was gay.

Dennis was, by all accounts, a dominant Golden Retriever and comments about his sexuality began to ring in his brain. If you remember, a dominant Golden Retriever's stronghold is **"I am who I am. I cannot change. I am hopeless."** As Dennis grew, this young tender Golden Retriever really started to believe in Satan's lie. As he entered high school, he started to entertain the thought that maybe he was gay even though at the time, the lifestyle was not in vogue as it is today. Thinking he was gay and living in a small farming town meant only one thing—don't let anyone know.

Now Dennis' parents were devoted Christians who like most in this small town went to church. At a young age, Dennis felt a strong connection with God. He would pray regularly and feel special in God's eyes. Dennis' first encounter with homosexuality came from the older boys in his church. These first encounters left him with a deep sense of shame. He had overheard some of the church leaders speak of how despicable this sin was. To Dennis, this was a sin God could not forgive. The stronghold continued to weigh in on his mind, "I am who I am, and I cannot change, I am hopeless."

By the time Dennis had reached his senior year in high school, his gift of playing the piano had warranted him a full musical scholarship to Oklahoma Baptist University, a prominent Christian university not far from his home. He was the first in his family to attend college. Dennis once again saw his chance for a new beginning. He wanted desperately to live according to God's precepts, and he knew his attraction to men was not God's intent. That first year at college was rough. He buried himself in his music and for fun, joined a glee club. There he met a girl named Melinda. He started to date her even though he had no physical attraction to her. He also met another student named Chuck who was straight. He so desperately wanted to live a straight life and he desperately wanted to put his homosexuality behind him.

About then, he met a prominent professor who seemed sincere and fatherly to Dennis. This "mentor" was well respected not only on campus, but in the community as well. He seemed to have a deep interest in Dennis, something no one really showed him before. After months of spending time with this professor in his office, restaurants, and coffee shops, Dennis started to feel safe enough to reveal his homosexuality in hopes the confession would bring healing. For a moment, as he confessed his attraction to men, it seemed as if the weight of the world was lifted from his shoulders. But that feeling quickly went away as his mentor revealed to him, he too was gay and wanted to start a relationship with him. Dennis ran. He couldn't understand why everyone was a fake, including himself.

At this point he gave up trying to be straight. The stronghold of the enemy was too strong; **"I am who I am. I cannot change. I am hopeless."** He broke his relationship off with Melinda and dove headlong into a homosexual relationship with another student on campus. His desire to have true intimacy was reduced to a small smoldering ember in his soul.

After a year of "getting nowhere with his music degree" and feeling the disgust of being in a homosexual relationship, he broke it off and dropped out of OBU. Feeling broken, he returned home to the farm. That is when he received a call from Chuck who was still going to OBU but living with his mom. "Dennis. I know this is going to sound strange, but I had a dream that God had used you to create thousands of worship songs for Him. I didn't think much of it until my mother said she had the same dream. I talked to my mom about this and we feel God is asking us to open our home to you. We will give you a room and a piano. All you have to do is pray and write songs. I know it sounds strange, but will you please consider our offer." Feeling he had nothing left to lose, Dennis accepted.

Once again, Dennis was hopeful, God was going to deliver him from his sin. He spent days writing and singing for the Lord right there in Chuck's house. Chuck began to sense and see the struggle Dennis was having with his sexuality.

Things came to a head one night as Chuck, being a sincere Christian, felt God calling him to talk to Dennis about his struggle. Chuck started to talk. "Dennis, I know you are struggling with homosexuality." When Dennis heard these words, the shame became so intense, he jumped up without thinking, ran out of the house and down the street. He was ashamed of the double standard he was living. And, based on how everything else had worked out in his life, he knew his friendship with Chuck was over.

Just about then, for some unknown reason, he stopped and looked up into the moonlit sky. What he saw were two clouds coming toward one another. One cloud was in the shape of Jesus with his arms open, the other was in the shape of a child. He sensed God was telling him, "Dennis, it's time to stop running and come to Me."

By then, Chuck, who was chasing Dennis, finally caught up to him. Dennis, sobbing uncontrollably, couldn't talk. Chuck, after gaining his breath, said, "Dennis, I don't know how to help you, but I know I know the Answer."

"What?" Dennis replied in bewilderment.

"I don't know how to help you, but I do know the Answer," said Chuck.

"What's that, Chuck?" Dennis asked flippantly.

"Well... the answer is Jesus," Chuck said.

Quickly Dennis responded, "Chuck, I've heard that my whole life. He [Jesus] hasn't done anything for me."

"Not like this you haven't," exclaimed Chuck. "You see, I believe Jesus is the Answer so much that here is what I'm willing to do. Would you be willing to walk toward Jesus with me? Whatever it takes, I guarantee you this, as long as I have breath, I will walk with you. If you fall down, I won't kick you, I won't mock you, I won't tell you 'I told you so.' I'll just help you up every time if you will let me. If you need a shoulder to cry on, I'm your guy. If you need someone to yell at when you don't know what to say, when you're so frustrated, yell at me. I can take it."

It was the very words Dennis needed to hear. He accepted Chuck's offer as a friend. Later Chuck was asked why he did what he did, especially in a time when most shied away from homosexuality. "I don't know why. I just wanted to be a friend that sticks closer than a brother."

In so many words, intimacy means "Into me you see". It is allowing to be seen for all the embarrassing things you hold deep within your soul. Many of us (including myself) fear intimacy because it requires me to be vulnerable with those things I'm most insecure with. My fear is that I can't trust this person with my shame. It is too embarrassing. For one to admit they masturbate, smoke marijuana, have sex, look at internet porn sites, think about turning gay, confessing they were raped or molested as a child, etc.... draws them into the scum of their shame.

The Good. The Bad. And the Ugly.

Let's face it, we all are made up of the good, the bad, and the ugly. No matter what it is, we all have it. Not being able to share my shame or ugliness with others out of fear I won't be accepted, however, puts me in a lonely place. Now I must pretend I'm not someone I am. I do this by putting on a mask to hide my "ugly." And it seems as if the mask I wear changes with the people around me. In front of my teacher I'm one way, when I hang around my friends after school, I'm another, and when I'm at home or with my friends at church I am yet another. I'm not sure who my friends like, me or the mask I wear. Uncertain of who I am, I begin lying about my identity to cover up what I think they won't like about me. My fear is that if my friends don't like me, they won't want to hang out with me and then I'd be all alone. Being like this, however, makes me feel all alone because I can't be who I really am. Instead, I must wear this mask and pretend I am one way when I'm really another.

What is your ugly? For me it has been my body. I've always been exceptionally thin and small. No matter how much I eat, I can't seem to keep the weight on. As a matter of fact, I didn't weigh 100 pounds until my sophomore year in high school. My desire was to have the body of an NFL linebacker because they are studs who get all the girls. Deep down inside, my heart longed for love. Even though I got the girl, to this day, I struggle with inadequate feelings of being a man because I weigh a mere 150 pounds. Little voices creep in my head saying, "You're not strong enough to be a man. You couldn't defend yourself and family against a flee."

So how does one get out of this mess of being someone they are not to keep their friends? TRUST! That's right, trust with a whole lot of courage wrapped around it. If you knew all of your friends were in the same boat as you, would it help? I'm going to let you in on a secret. Most of the people you know at your school, in church, and to some degree even at home, are all wearing a mask to hide their ugly. They too are like you and I in that they long for acceptance and approval, so they pretend to be who they think they need to be.

Now I want you to think of your best friend. What is it that makes your best friend your best friend? Can you tell him or her your deepest darkest secrets and know they won't judge you for your faults? Would they cover your back? Would they be there for you in times of need? Do you respect their opinion and advice? Do they respect yours? If the answer is yes, then you know what it means to be intimate. You also know what true freedom feels like. Now if you don't have a friend like that, don't feel bad, you aren't alone. Many of us go through life longing for deep meaningful relationships yet never find them. It is the way God wired us. We can't help but desire to be loved, approved of, and accepted.

What would the world look like if you could have not just one friend that accepts you for who you are, but many friends? Wouldn't it be awesome if you could show your ugly and know it wouldn't be held against you? Imagine the freedom you'd feel knowing no matter how embarrassing and unsettling your situation was, no one would judge you and all would be there to support you. You could literally be who you are, the real you.

So how do we do this? The Bible says we must give in order to receive. So, the first step down the intimacy path begins with you giving to another by being vulnerable. That is how it started with your best friend. Either you or he/she got real, and the rest was history. That's the way it works. All relationships follow a similar path. Not all, however, reach its final destination of being truly transparent and feeling love and acceptance. This is the road we must all choose to feel and be loved. It requires risk, vulnerability, and courage. It requires you to take your mask off and be transparent. This is the giving part of the equation. You give your transparency so that you can receive your friend's transparency. Or, another way of saying it, you give your trust so that you can receive your friend's trust.

The Path

It had been two and a half days, and some forty miles of hard travel over the Samaritan Hills to a small well just outside of town. Reports had come in from Galilee just a few days earlier that John the Baptist was taken into custody by the Jews. It was customary as a Jew to cross the Jordan and travel along the east side of the river to avoid any contact with unclean Samaritans. So, when Jesus chose the most direct route of walking right through the heart of Samaria, it left many of his disciples feeling awkward. All they could figure was that He chose the quickest route to reach Galilee as soon as possible. What His disciples didn't know was Jesus had an ulterior motive; an appointment with a woman by noon. So, they pushed hard to meet her. By the time they had reached the well, they were tired, hungry, and thirsty, so Jesus sent them into Sychar, a small town of only a half mile to the north, for food and drink. Meanwhile Jesus sat alongside the well waiting.

A woman in her mid to late twenties arrived. She was quiet and to herself, not wanting to be bothered or noticed. She looked shameful and embarrassed as if a small voice inside her head was continually pounding on her significance. She seemed a bit perplexed as to why a Jewish man would be sitting beside this well, but she didn't want to draw attention to herself. So, she quietly went about her work, keeping her head down, not wanting to be bothered.

As she began to draw water, He spoke, breaking the uncomfortable silence. "Would you give me a drink of water?" He asked? She wanted to hide. She had no desire to entertain conversation with some self-righteous Jew. Besides, she knew it was unlawful for a Jew to drink of a Samaritan cup. "How come you, a Jew, are asking me, a Samaritan woman, for a drink?" she asked in desperation to get this man to leave her alone. Jesus answered, "If you knew the generosity of God and who I am, you would be asking me for a drink, and I would give you fresh, living water."

Still feeling uncomfortable speaking to this man, she made another attempt to deaden the conversation. "Sir, you don't even have a bucket to draw with, and this well is deep. So how are you going to get this 'living water'?" Hoping to provoke Him into leaving her alone she added, "Are you a better man than our ancestor Jacob, who dug this well and drank from it, he and his sons and livestock, and passed it down to us?"

Understanding her self-conscious feelings of insignificance, Jesus looked right into her eyes and answered with a tender passion she had only seen from her mother as a child, "Everyone who drinks this water will get thirsty again and again. Anyone who drinks the water I give will never thirst—not ever. The water I give will be an artesian spring within, gushing fountains of endless life." Somewhat confused yet intrigued by His answer, her disposition began to change. She thought to herself, *'Living water?' What is He talking about? I don't get this man. Why is He even talking to me? I'm a nobody. I'm a Samaritan. Jews hate Samaritans. I'm fat and ugly, living in poverty with some guy I call my boyfriend. I'm about as unclean and dirty as one can get. If He knew this, He wouldn't want to even be seen talking to me let alone offering me His 'living water.' But, if what He is telling me is true, then I'll never have to embarrass myself in front of all these people by coming to this well every day.* "Sir, give me this water so I won't ever get thirsty, won't ever have to come back to this well again!"

Sensing her intrigue, Jesus draws closer to her. Now only a foot away, and with his eyes focused on hers, gently, he speaks, "Go call your husband and then come back." Her eyes drop away. She thinks, *Why does he need my husband? How embarrassing. Is this a trick? Did someone tell him I'm living with some guy so I don't have to live on the street?* Somewhat ashamed, she looks up and mocks, "I have no husband."

Perfectly orchestrated by Jesus, He now is given the opportunity to enter into her ugliness and shame and show her He loves her just the way she is. After all, this is His daughter. He has walked with her every day of her life. He has felt every pain and disappointment she has felt. He leans in, again looking right into her eyes and speaks,

"That's nicely put, 'I have no husband.' You've had five husbands, and the man you're living with now isn't even your husband." Her defenses shoot up as she tries to maintain some dignity. *How does he...? He must be a prophet! I'm speaking to a prophet!* Quickly, she tries to skirt the issue. "Oh, so you're a prophet! Well, tell me this: Our ancestors worshiped God at this mountain, but you Jews insist that Jerusalem is the only place for worship, right?"

Now realizing He has earned the right to be heard, He speaks, "Believe me, woman, the time is coming when you Samaritans will worship the Father neither here at this mountain nor there in Jerusalem. You worship guessing in the dark; we Jews worship in the clear light of day. God's way of salvation is made available throughout the Jews. But the time is coming—it has, in fact, come—when what you're called will not matter and where you go to worship will not matter."

He has captured her full attention, more importantly, reached into her heart and held her significance in his hand. Realizing this, she begins to feel a love and acceptance she has never felt before. The condemning voices begin to quiet. This man she felt so self-critical of was now telling her she was worthy of worshiping His God. This is all any Samaritan has ever wanted, to be equal to the Jews. No Jew had ever spoken such words of acceptance to her before.

Now, standing still with her bucket in hand, he continues to speak. "It is who you are and the way you live that counts before God. Your worship must engage your spirit in the pursuit of truth. That's the kind of people the Father is out looking for, those who are simply and honestly *themselves* before him in their worship. God is sheer being itself—Spirit. Those who worship him must do it out of their very being, their spirits, their true selves, in adoration."

Not knowing if she could put all her trust in what He just said, she retorted, "I don't know about that. I do know that the Messiah is coming *to save me from this wretched life.* When he arrives, we'll get the whole story."

"I am He," said Jesus. "You don't have to wait any longer or look any further."

Just then the disciples came back. They were shocked to see Jesus talking to a woman everyone in town was too ashamed to address. No one said what they were thinking, but their faces certainly showed it.

The woman took the hint and quickly walked away. In her hurried state, she forgot her water pot. Back in the village her hope overwhelmed her. Her shame to speak to the others all but gone. She had been forgiven by the Messiah Himself and couldn't help but tell everyone, "Come see a man who knew all about the things I did, who knows me inside and out. Do you think this could be the Messiah?" And they went out to see for themselves.

Have you ever found yourself feeling inadequate to talk to strangers in your school about Jesus? You cringe at the thought of expressing your beliefs about Jesus to someone you don't know or trust. Society tells us it's okay to believe in whatever we want, but it's not okay to impose those beliefs on others. Yet you keep hearing your youth pastor tell you of the great youth group commission and how we as Christians are to go into all the hallways of your school making disciples of all classmen and bringing them to all youth group functions. You know how cruel peers can be and you know how cool Christ is for you, but you just aren't sure if you're willing to impose your beliefs on others for fear you'll be ridiculed and outcast.

How did Jesus capture the attention of a woman who had no desire to talk to Him? Think about it. Jesus is a Jew going into an area of the world where people despise Jews. He begins a conversation with a woman who dressed and acted like she didn't care about herself or Him. Jesus was able to break down all of these barriers and get to her heart. I know, you are thinking, *but that's Jesus. He can do stuff like that because he is God. I'm not. I don't think I could walk onto the campus of my rival school and share Jesus with the quarterback of the football team.*

But you could, if you understood the path one must take to reach into the heart of another. You see all relationships follow the same path whether they take twenty minutes to develop, or twenty years. Jesus may have been God in the flesh, but he made one thing perfectly clear: He was human. He wanted to model to us how we could be like Him. So, He did away with all His Godly powers to show us how we could live like Him.

Steps to Intimacy

Accomplice
Acquaintance
Friend
Close Friend
True Friend

At any time, if you were to look at any relationship you are in, it would fall into one of five categories. You would be an accomplice, acquaintance, friend, close friend, or true friend. If you are an accomplice to someone, you are accomplishing something together with that person. Maybe you are taking a class together, in a club, or even in the same youth group. These are those you've never met or haven't been formally introduced to. An accomplice is the most distant form of relationship there is. When the woman at the well arrived to draw water, she and Jesus were accomplices because they were at the well together both needing water to drink.

The next step down the road of intimacy is to become an acquaintance. An acquaintance is someone you have engaged in conversation with. You know their name and a few details of their life, but you wouldn't consider them a friend. Again, this might be someone you see in youth group, have geometry with, play sports with, or see on Facebook or Instagram from time to time, but you don't hang out with him/her any other time. As soon as Jesus struck up a conversation with the woman, he became acquainted with her and she with Him.

The next step down the road to intimacy is that of a friend. We all have two types of friends: close and distant. Another way of putting this is we have our inner circle of friends and our outer circle. Those we call friend, are those we hang out with because they are fun or have some common interest, but we still don't know their deep dark secrets, nor do they know ours. This is where the mask thing shows up; what they know of you, they like. These would be those you respond to on Instagram, shoot a text to occasionally, or talk to in class or youth group. Most of the talk is small and superficial. Jesus became a friend to the woman at the well when she started to entertain conversation with him instead of just trying to blow him off. How big can this circle grow? It really depends on how much time you want to commit to these friends of yours. If you are committed to texting them every so often or commenting on their posts, you could have a lot of friends. I've known some to have over 50 friends like this. That's a big circle.

A close friend is one you hang out with all the time. Someone you've come to trust and respect. And you know they trust and respect you because they ask for your advice often. Usually, you share at least one thing in common with them, which is how you bonded in the first place. You care about him/her and would be there for him/her if he/she were in trouble. You know it and they know it. If you look at the relationship Jesus had with the woman at the well, He approached this category by giving her words of acceptance and encouragement as a Samaritan woman. He was letting her know he cared for her just the way she was.

The final step to being intimate with someone is called being a true friend. A true friend is someone you haven't hidden anything from. Someone you have enough trust in to let them see you for who you really are. Your best friends may have seen your **bad**, but your true friends have seen your **ugly.** There are no masks at this point.

Another quality of a true friend is someone who cares enough about you to call you on your sin. They know when you are covering up lies and they are not afraid to let you know how they see you in your circumstance or situation. They aren't doing it to belittle you, or to embarrass you, but instead because they hate to see you suffer from the consequences of your actions. Jesus reached this point when he called this woman on her promiscuous lifestyle. He knew it was her ugly. He knew this is why she shamefully showed up at noon when all the rest of the women in town showed up early in the morning. He knew her promiscuous life was the talk of all the women in town. He knew it was the source of her pain. He knew she longed for acceptance and approval, and He cared enough to tell her all her life she was looking in all the wrong places to fill her void. In fact, He went on to give her hope in Him. **True friends give hope.**

Not many of us have true friends. We all long for them, but rarely do we have the courage to let someone in to see the ugliness that lives inside. We'd rather stay closed for fear no one would want us for who we are. Jesus desires to see you have true friendships in your life. I am here to say you can if you choose to be honest with who you are. You, like everyone else, are not good, bad, or ugly, but a combination of all three. This is the crux of this book. Do you want to give hope to a hopeless world? Then you are going to have to walk this path and get transparent with some of your friends. This means respectfully taking chances when others won't. This means humbling yourself and speaking about what isn't working for you in your life to those you trust will listen.

Earning the right to be heard means placing yourself in a position where you are respected enough for your friend to listen to what you have to say. Pastor John Maxwell once said, "People don't care how much you know until they know how much you care." When looking back at Jesus' meeting with this woman, we see a Man not giving up or giving in to this woman's desire to be left alone. The conversation is awkward and uncomfortable at first, but that is okay. His desire to reach her comes out of His compassion for her. He knows her life sucks, and He also knows she feels stuck in her fears, flaws, and failures. He knows if He can break these strongholds in her mind, He can set her free (Philippians. 4:6-8; 2 Corinthians 10:3-5).

Like many of us, she lacks confidence in herself. She bought the lie that she was a loser and there was nothing she could do to change that. What she needed was someone who would fight for her. Someone who was willing to stand for a greater possibility in her life. Someone who was willing to believe in her more than she believed in herself (Ephesians 2:4-10). Someone who was willing to fight for each level of intimacy, because He cared.

If you remember the story that started this chapter, isn't this what Chuck did for Dennis? To be a true friend means you must be willing to let things get a little messy. Maybe some contentious words fly in a heated conversation? Or maybe, as in the case of Chuck and Dennis, intense deep dark secrets flush up to the surface and must be dealt with. Regardless of the circumstance, there is a deep-seated commitment to stand with and for your friend.

You've heard the verse, "Greater love has no one than this, that someone lay down his life for his friends." (John 15:13) *The Message* by Eugene Peterson says it this way, "Put your life on the line for your friends." This may mean sticking up for your friend when he/she is being treated unfairly. It also means, sticking up for your friend when he/she is doing something wrong. James nailed it when he wrote, "Therefore, to him (or her) who knows to do good, and does not do it, to him (or her) it is sin." Ouch! That one hurts. You mean, I have to talk about things I see in my brother or sister that maybe they don't even see in themselves? But what if they get mad, or worse, never want to speak to me again?

How often have we known someone whose life sucks? We can see their pain and discomfort, but because we don't know them well enough or feel it's not our right, we don't say or do anything to help them. And life goes on. Nothing changes, or things get worse. And we feel we've let God down, heaping guilt on ourselves for not being able to do anything.

If we take the lead of Christ, then we are going to have to walk the path one step at a time. Each step comes with vulnerability and compassion. It's called humility. Now, let me show you how this works.

The Initiate-Reciprocate Phenomenon

If you want to go from being an accomplice to an acquaintance, you're going to have to make the first move and start asking questions to find common ground between you and this person. If you want to go from an acquaintance to a friend, you're going to have to invite them to do things that they like doing. You're going to have to extend yourself to them in such a way that they get you like hanging out with them. If you want them to become part of your close friends, you are going to have to confide in them, respect their opinion, be vulnerable and trust them with your secrets. And finally, if you want them to be a true friend, like a brother or sister, you are going to have to take your mask off. You are going to have to be bold, and risk letting them know you and all the embarrassing shameful things you don't let anyone else know. If you want a true friend, then you're going to have to be a true friend. In each case or step, you are going to have to make the first move. But wait. There is something else to this God-created formula.

Do not skip steps! In your desire to have deep meaningful relationships it is tempting to dive too deep too soon. Do not go from being an acquaintance to a true friend. This is too big of a jump and trust in the relationship hasn't been developed. Jesus may have walked this path with the woman at the well in ten minutes, but for most of us, this path could take months, maybe even years to develop.

So how do you know when they are ready to move to the next step? Simple, they will let you know when they reciprocate your actions. In other words, if they start asking you questions about you, you've just gone from being an accomplice to an acquaintance. When they start inviting you to hang out with their group of friends, then you know you are now a friend. When they invite you to do something one on one, and begin to confide in you, then you know you are a close friend. Finally, when they come to you to talk about a problem, you've entered their inner circle, and when they begin to show you the embarrassing pain in their life, then you'll know you have a true friend. It is at this point you've earned the right to be heard. It is also at this point you can share your beliefs in Christ in a genuine way, and they will be willing to listen because they know you care.

Finally, don't expect this person to reciprocate every time you initiate. This trust thing is never a straight line. Sometimes you'll get a yes and sometimes you won't. That's okay. I don't do everything my friends ask or want me to do. I have other commitments and it just isn't feasible for me to say yes to everyone all the time. I certainly hope my friends understand and aren't offended because I say no to them. So please, realize if they say no, they aren't doing it to hurt your feelings.

We started this chapter learning of a young man named Chuck who had a heart for a friend struggling with his sexual identity. It was an amazing story of courage as one brother in Christ stood for another. Next, we learned of how intentional Christ was when He showed us how to walk the steps of intimacy with a young Samaritan woman at the well. We then learned how we could be like Christ and walk through these steps to become a true friend and impact other's lives. Finally, we learned of the risks we must take to go deeper in our friendships. In the next chapter, we will be learning of the one thing that atheists struggle to explain—love.

Now it is time to get with your mentor and go over this chapter. He or she may have another challenge for you. If so, you can do this! May the Force be with you.

QUOTABLES:

"Intimacy means 'in-to-me-you-see.' It is the natural result of growing close." Jean-Marie Jobs

NOTABLES:

Dennis Jernigan went on to become one of the most prolific worship song writers of all time, writing over one thousand worship songs sung in churches all over the world. To this day, he continues to do the work of God as he has created a ministry to lead young men and women out of their homosexual addiction and back into a heterosexual life. You can learn more of his life in a documentary titled, *Dennis Jernigan, Sing Over*

Me by Free Verse Films. To learn more of Dennis' story and ministry visit www.SingOverMeMovie.com For your viewing pleasure, you can watch the trailer here: http://bit.ly/Sing_Over_Me_Trailer

6

LOVE IS A LEAP

They say it's a blessing
They say it's a gift
They say it's a miracle and I believe that it is
It conquers all
but it's a mystery
Love breaks your heart
Love takes no less than everything
Love makes it hard
And it fades away so easily.

Vanessa Williams/Brian McKnight, Love Is

'Tis better to have loved and lost than never to have loved at all.

Alfred Lord Tennyson

A new command I give to you, that you love one another, even as I have loved you, that you also love one another.

John 13:34

It seems every Olympics has a golden moment. A story of captivating courage and inspiration that touches the hearts of all who watch. A moment that stays transfixed in our minds forever. In 2016, a white haired South African who had spent 50 years coaching world class track athletes finally saw one of her protégé win gold. His name was Wayde Van Niekerk, and at 24 years old he demolished a 17-year-old world record in the men's 400-meter race. What makes this story so compelling is the healing this young athlete brought to his country. For years, this 74-year-old coach had seen world class talent come her way. The only problem was none could compete in the Olympics because of her country's Apartheid (segregation) laws. "I had quite a few top top athletes with so much God given talents and they never had the opportunity or the privilege to take part outside the boarders of South Africa. With the weight of his country squarely on his shoulders, Van Niekerk became the first South African to win Gold at the Olympic Games. Back home, both Black and White celebrated in the streets.

http://bit.ly/Van_Niekerk_Wins
http://bit.ly/Niekerk_Gives_God_the_Glory

Or how about Eric Moussambani, the young Equatorial Guinea swimmer in the 2000 Sidney Olympics. Learning to swim only months earlier, he risked his life to live a dream. As fans hopelessly watched for what seemed to be an eternity, young Eric flailed in the water attempting to swim. As he slowly made it across the pool, those in the stands began cheering him on. The cheering became louder and louder as if they were trying to will young Eric to the finish. Finally, after

1 minute and 52 seconds of what we would call near drowning, he reached his goal, his destiny, his feat of the impossible, and with it a lesson to the world that victory can only be found to those who hold back nothing and risk it all.

http://bit.ly/Eric_Moussambani

As much as these stories captivated the true meaning of the Olympic spirit, nothing gripped the heart more than in 1992 at the Barcelona Games when the world not only took witness of courage, but of love as well. His name was Derek Redmond, and Great Britain had selected him as their premier runner for the 400-meter race. Many experts favored young Derek to win the Gold, and many who followed his sport hoped he would.

Just four years earlier, young Derek found himself pulling out of the Seoul, Korea Olympics with bilateral Achilles tendon problems. Now, after five operations and four more years of dedicated training, Derek Redmond once again found himself representing his country and favored to win in the Olympics.

In the first two rounds of qualifying for the semifinals, Derek had marked his two fastest times in five years. Finally, he was getting the chance to show the world what he could do. Then, it happened.

Rounding turn three of his semifinal race, Derek felt a pop; his hamstring had torn. He fell to the ground in obvious agony. It was then that this story of courage and love began. "It dawned on me I was out of the Olympic final," he said. "I just wanted to finish the race." Redmond struggled to his feet and began to hobble for the finish line all alone on the track. Determined to finish, Derek continued to hobble in obvious pain. And now with each agonizing step, eighty thousand people began to realize the determination and courage that lay in Derek Redmond's heart. They stood and began to cheer him on.

Jim Redmond, Derek's father, seated high in the stands at Olympic Stadium wearing a T-shirt that said "Have you hugged your foot today?" and a cap that said, "Just Do It," did what any loving father would do. It didn't seem to matter to Jim that we live in a day when authorities put in place systems of security that seem impenetrable. All he knew was his child needed him. "I was thinking I had to get him there, so he could say he finished the semifinal race." If anyone knew of Derek's agonizing past, it was his father. For eight years, Derek had sacrificed his life for the chance to be an Olympic champion. As a father, Jim could not just sit idly by.

Climbing the wall that separated spectators from participants, Jim caught up to his son who was about to stop because the pain was unbearable. "We are going to finish this race," he told young Derek. With determined eyes fixed on the finish line some one hundred yards away, the stoic father grabbed ahold of his son's left arm and placed it over his shoulder, and the two began to walk. Melting into his father's arms, Derek laid his head on his father's shoulder and began to cry. Officials attempted to intercede, but the staunch father was not going to let go of his son. "I wasn't going to be stopped by anything," the older Redmond said. And with each step the two took, the roar of the crowd got louder. Father and son, arm in arm, together they crossed the finish line.

http://bit.ly/Derek_Redmond

Commitment, Promise, and Love

What is love? Have you ever sat down and really tried to answer this question? Is it something you feel? Or does it have nothing to do with feelings? Is it something you express physically through sexual contact, or can it be expressed in other ways? Is it some mystical thing we somehow acquire, or is it some tangible thing that takes effort and intention to acquire? Why is it something we all seem to crave, yet in its simplest form we struggle to express? Why does it make some people like Jim Redmond do the extraordinary? Why does loving your mom and dad seem so much different than loving your boyfriend or girlfriend?

The problem with love is that it is hard to grasp. I love hot dogs and I love my wife, yet I eat hot dogs and throw away the wrapper. So which love is the real love? Hollywood's hot and sticky version of love is simple — it's a feeling heightened by physical touch. Could love be an emotion that may be here today and gone tomorrow? Or is this a counterfeit to true love? Listen to what Paul writes in his first letter to the Corinthians.

> Love is patient, love is kind and is not jealous; love does not brag and is not arrogant, does not act unbecomingly; it does not seek its own, is not provoked, does not take into account a wrong suffered, does not rejoice in unrighteousness, but rejoices with the truth; bears all things, believes all things, hopes all things, endures all things. Love never fails.
>
> 1 Corinthians 13:4-8

What does it mean to be loving toward your friends and family as Christ would? This wouldn't be nearly as hard to pull off if people weren't so strange, yet we see their quirks and weirdness and find it difficult to love them.

How do you know someone loves you? I mean really loves you. Is it something they say? How often have you heard your friend tell you she knows her boyfriend loves her cause he says so, then a week or two later he's broken it off? Can we really say a person loves you just because he or she says so? Someone once told me love is a verb. This means love is an action, it is quantified in what we do for another and not what we say. What precedes actions are promises. **Promises are the key to love**.

Let's say you notice Grandma's windows are looking dirty, so you decide to help her out and clean them this Saturday. You call her up to make sure she'll be there, and you promise her you'll come over in the morning to clean her windows. Is this love? Not yet. You've just made a promise in words that you are going to help her out. Love comes when you actually go over and clean her windows. It is at this point your grandma gets your love.

Now, let's say Saturday comes and you forget the promise you made to your grandma. You've now just told your grandma how much you love her as she sits and waits for you to come. Either way, once a promise is made, it declares a commitment of love. So, the key to loving someone lies in the promises you keep. And the key to someone loving you lies in the promises they keep.

The Physical Universe Doesn't Lie

Think back to a time when someone close to you broke a promise to take you somewhere or buy you something. Do you remember how excited you got waiting for that moment to arrive, only to have your heart broken because they didn't show? Do you remember how rejected, insignificant, and small you felt?

When I was a senior in high school, I played left field for my high school baseball team. Then, baseball was my life; I was devoting numerous hours every afternoon and traveling every weekend with a team. The only thing that kept me in the line-up was my heart. Diving after balls hit into the outfield, sliding into bases headfirst were just a couple of the things I did to stay in the game. I struggled to play at the high school level and knew my desire to be drafted or receive a scholarship to a four-year university was highly unlikely. As my final season wore on, I started to realize my dad hadn't once seen me play. So, I started asking him if he'd come to my games. Every time he promised he would, and every time, it seemed there was yet another excuse as to why he didn't show. I excused it off saying my dad was working hard to provide for the family, so who was I to interfere (If you think I struggled with my self-worth in high school you'd be correct). Finally, we were to play our last game at home, so I begged my dad to come see me play. I told him it would probably be my last game, and I really wanted him to see me play. He looked right into my eyes and promised he would be there.

I was convinced my dad would show. It made me feel important to think my dad would take the time out of his busy schedule to watch me play a meaningless high school baseball game. During warm ups, I kept looking into the parking lot for his car to arrive; it didn't. The game started, and he still hadn't arrived. I kept thinking to myself, "He'll come, he's just running late as usual." As the game progressed, my expectations started to dim, yet I kept hoping. Just before my last at bat, I remember telling myself, "If he comes now, at least he'll be able to see me hit for the last time." My dad never came. He forgot, and with it he communicated to me how much he loved me. Satan's lie that lived deep within my subconscious was strengthened that day; I wasn't important enough to be loved.

Broken Promises... A Cry for Help

If you think my dad didn't show up because he wanted to crush my spirit, think again. When someone breaks a promise with you, it isn't because they are inherently evil and desire to hurt you. No, it's because there are other things in their life that are getting in the way of what is important.

Anytime someone breaks a promise with you, it truly is a cry for help. Something is wrong. Is this not true for you? What if you did forget the promise you made to Grandma, and didn't show to clean her windows? Don't you think something has to be eating at you enough for you to totally forget your own promise to your grandma? Did you break the promise because you are evil, and you want your grandma to feel disappointment, abandonment, and pain? No, you broke the promise because something else was more important or urgent than your relationship with Grandma.

There are two types of promises in the world, implied and expressed. Implied promises are promises that go without saying. Dad or mom don't have to sit you down and say, "Now son, as your parent, I promise to clothe you, and feed you, and put a roof over your head until you are eighteen." No, those are promises they made to you the day you were conceived.

Unfortunately, some of you don't have your biological dad or mom raising you, and you know the disappointment and pain you feel because of it. It was a promise that was broken a long time ago. It was also a huge cry for help. Other implied promises show up when you enroll into an activity, sport, or school. You promise to show up on time to learn while your teacher, instructor, or coach promises to show up on time to teach.

Expressed promises, on the other hand, are promises you speak to another, like telling your grandma you'll wash her windows, or telling your friend you'll give them a call.

Forgiveness: God's Cure to Broken Promises

How many times have you heard, "I'm sorry," when a friend or family member breaks a promise with you? Does it really take away the disappointment you feel deep in your heart? More than likely, it depends on how the person is saying it more so than what is being said. Remember, actions speak louder than words. So, if someone is humbly coming before you with a repentant heart knowing they messed up and caused you pain, you will know they truly feel sorry for what they've done.

According to Daniel Tochinni in his book, *Killing the Victim before the Victim Kills You: Building Relationships Through Keeping Promises*, the words "I'm sorry," is one person's way of excusing themselves from their hurtful behavior. By accepting their apology, you are giving them license to do it again. How many times have you heard the guy who cheated on his girlfriend tell her "I'm sorry" and she takes him back? Don't you just shake your head and think she's a fool, he's going to do it again and she just excused him for his wrongful actions? Forgiveness, on the other hand, is a gift from the one who broke the promise to the one the promise was broken to. Now which would you rather give—a gift or an excuse?

To sum this up, let's revisit the story of Jim Redmond and his son Derek. As his father, Jim had made an implied promise to protect, provide, and teach Derek how to be a man. So, when Derek fell, Jim knew Derek's dream to be an Olympic champion was shattered. And as a father who loved his child, he needed to be there for him. As he jumped over the rail and onto the track, Jim realized his son wasn't going to make it if he didn't come alongside of him to help. As a loving father who stood by his son's side through eight grueling years of training, he had to help his son finish that race. "I wasn't going to be stopped by anything," he told reporters. Can promise and love get any clearer?

Expectation: Satan's Strategy to Suffocate Love

What happens to love when someone expects more than what another is willing to offer? That's right. It kills it. Imagine if Derek Redmond said to his father when Jim finally caught up to him, "Where have you been? Can't you see I'm in pain? Why weren't you here sooner? I can't believe you are so insensitive to my needs." Or, what if Grandma said, "Thanks for doing my windows, but I can't see much improvement. Now I'm going to have to clean them myself. I don't even know why you kids try to help me out. It just ends up being more work for me."

One day my boys, who were five and seven years old at the time, wanted to help me stain a loft bed I was building them. Their intentions were to give out of love and help their daddy. I, on the other hand, envisioned stain being spilled everywhere with the result being a bad-looking job. My comments were harsh. "No don't put it on there, put it on here. Okay. Stop! Wait a second! You aren't doing it right. Let me show you how to do it" (like I'm a professional furniture maker).

After ten minutes of Daddy frantically badgering his sons to stain the wood the way he wanted it done, the boys said they were done. It only took Daddy ten minutes to kill their act of love with expectations. Daddy was crushed moments later when God spoke this truth into his heart: "Why can't you control your kids less, and let your kids love you more?" Daddy went back to his boys and asked them for forgiveness. It kind of went like this. "Luke and Dominic, will you please forgive Daddy for being so harsh with you when you just wanted to help me stain your new bed? I realize now, all you wanted to do was help Daddy, and Daddy made it so difficult for you. You guys are awesome stainers and I didn't mean to hurt your feelings." What do you think they said when they saw tears coming down Daddy's face? Thank God reconciliation is just one request for forgiveness away.

Satan understands the power of love. He cannot have it. It draws people closer together. So, he works extra hard at creating a society where people feel entitled (another word for expectation) to have certain things regardless of the effect it may have on their neighbor. This type of nurturing creates greed, lust and taking rather than selflessness, giving, and love.

Now the big question. Who do you love? Who are you willing to put before yourself? Is it Grandma on Saturday? Maybe a sister or brother? What act of kindness could you selflessly do for them? All God wants of you is to love without expectation. Can you do that?

Love Comes in Five Languages

I wish I could say all you need to do is a random act of kindness and the recipient would feel your love. Unfortunately, love is a little more complicated than that. Studies seem to indicate we all have a unique way we communicate love. According to Dr. Gary Chapman, a renowned marriage and family counselor, types of love can be categorized into five unique areas: quality time, acts of service, words of affirmation, receiving gifts, and physical touch. He calls these the five love languages. The common denominator to each is time and attention.

Now back to Grandma. If acts of service is number one on her list, then washing her dirty windows will be a huge act of love. Let's say, however, acts of service is not her love language but quality time is, then cleaning her dirty windows won't tell her you love her as loud as sitting down with her to play a game of cards. Don't get me wrong, you can still show her you love her by doing her windows, it just might not resonate as deep in her heart.

Here's the deal. If you want someone to truly know you care, then figure out their love language and develop promises with them that speak that language. If Grandma loves gifts, tell her you have a surprise gift for her and want to meet up with her on Saturday morning, then go buy her flowers. If it is words of affirmation, write her a letter affirming her of how much you appreciate her as your grandma. If it is physical touch, promise her a walk Saturday morning and hold her hand while doing so. Hold to the promises you make. After all, isn't that how Christ loves us? As a Christian, love isn't a thing, it is *the* thing. It isn't something you do; it is the very reason you are here. This is why Christ summed up all the law and the prophets by saying, "Love the Lord your God with all your heart, soul, mind and strength" and "Love your neighbor as yourself." (Mark 12:30-31)

Love is the most powerful force around, and God has entrusted it to you. Its true potential, its true power can only be expressed when you realize it is not for you to have but to give. And, when you break a promise, or someone breaks a promise to you, listen for the cry. It will tell you a lot about what isn't working in your or their life.

We started this chapter with a story of a father who could not stand idly by watching his son suffer. He had to do something simply because he was his father. We learned that promises, whether expressed or implied, are the key to loving another. Next, we looked at how Satan works to stop love with expectation and entitlement. Finally, we learned of the five love languages and how important it is to know what love language others speak so that we may better serve them. I hope by now you know the difference between loving hot dogs and loving your mom or dad. In the next chapter, we are going to learn of the most powerful divine secret God has ever given and how you can use it to change the world.

It is now time to get with your mentor and go over this chapter. He or she may have another challenge for you. Remember, the Force is with you

7

THE ULTIMATE ACT OF HUMILITY

The Saint who advances on his knees never retreats.

Jim Elliot

God is only after two things for your life—that you be happy and holy. And He knows that you cannot be really happy until you are holy.

Winkie Pratney

I want to introduce you to someone who understands the power of prayer. His name is Kyle. As a senior going to Steele Canyon High School in Spring Valley, California, he needed wheels. You see, along with school, Kyle participated on three different Christian EMO Core X bands as a drummer, lead guitarist, and lead vocalist. With school, bands, and many other extracurricular activities, Kyle's life was busy.

So was his mom's. Without a car, Kyle was left searching for ways to get to band practices, church activities, and school. Most of the chore of driving Kyle landed squarely on mom's shoulders (sound familiar?). Unfortunately, his parents couldn't buy Kyle a car, and although Kyle had a license to drive, he didn't have any money to buy himself a set of wheels. So, he did what every other Christian teen in need of a car without money does— pray and pray and pray some more.

God finally answered his prayers. Kyle and his band were asked to perform at a high school youth group kick off for the school year. What Kyle did not know was that one of the youth group leaders had donated his car to the church and the church was going to raffle off this car to some lucky student. Other items were being raffled as well, but the car was the headline and it drew a crowd. Students who didn't even belong to the youth group came in hopes they would drive home in their own car.

The evening finally came to a close. Kyle and his band were a hit. Worship was awesome, and the raffle was a great success. The only item left to raffle was the car. Kyle's drummer did a great drum role as the youth pastor pulled the final ticket. As he read the number, you could hear groans, but no excited high school student jumping up and down yelling, "I won, I won." The youth pastor again read the number, and no one came forward. So... he had no choice but to pull another lucky ticket. Can you believe it happened again? No one came forward.

Again, the youth pastor, seeming a bit concerned, decided to draw one final time. Again, the drum rolled, and the ticket was drawn. This time it was Kyle's number and he went crazy. He had been praying hard for this moment for at least a year, and God came through. He couldn't wait to tell his mom. He knew her prayers were answered as well.

Why Pray?

Have you ever asked yourself why pray? Think about it. If every day of your life has been ordained and written in a book before you were born (Psalm 139), and He knows your heart before you do (Jeremiah 17:9-10), then what good will praying do? He already knows what you are going to pray for. He has heard your prayer through your heart well before it has reached your lips, yet the Bible is littered with scripture that tells us the most vital weapon we have against the enemy is prayer (Ephesians 6:18-19).

The next question that must be asked then is who is the act of prayer for, you or God? If He already knows your prayer before you lift it to Him (Psalm 139:4), then I'd venture to guess this thing called prayer is more for you than Him.

Praying is the ultimate act of humility. Being on your knees before God acknowledges two things: He is your Creator and you are reliant on Him for everything you have (including your next breath). By going to Him with your requests, you are acknowledging He is the one who has the power over everything in your world. This is called humility.

This is why God calls us to pray. It is the way in which you stay in relationship with Him. Matter of fact, just as you can be at different stages of intimacy with friends, so too can you be at different stages of intimacy with God. The more vulnerable and real you become with Him, the more vulnerable and real He becomes with you. Your prayer life determines your level of vulnerability with God.

God designed you to pray. It is through your prayers that you have a relationship with God. It is through your prayers that you call upon Him to fight against the forces of evil in your world. It is through your prayers that you help others. It is through your prayers God shows Himself. When you pray, God moves.

Now let's peel back the layers of this onion and look at it a bit more closely. What if you decided you weren't going to pray? After all, God knows what is on your heart, and He knows what is best for you. Would He not become some distant orchestrator in the heavens that really could not be known? More importantly, how quickly would you be able to discern His small quiet voice when He speaks? And what would happen if you were hoping, like Kyle, for a car, yet never got one? Does this mean God doesn't care about you? After all, you are not praying to Him and it doesn't seem like He is concerned about your life. Would this leave you feeling as if you need to make things happen in your life rather than being reliant on God? And where is God now? Now that you've decided to be self-reliant.

Do you see the slippery slope not praying creates? There is only one reason a Christian doesn't pray, and it is called pride. That's right, self-reliance is a severe form of pride and it severely forces a wedge between you and God. I know, I've been there, and it isn't fun.

Do you know what is fun? Praying to Him daily and listening for His voice. Waiting on Him to direct you and being obedient to His call. Praying on behalf of your friends and seeing Him work in their lives. I can't begin to tell you how crazy fun life becomes when you start praying this way. Prayer is the ultimate act of communion with your God. If you don't do it, you are missing out. Just set 15 minutes of your day aside for prayer. Keep a journal of your requests and go back into it when you get an answer. By keeping a list of answered prayers, you'll really start to see how God is working in your life.

I love praying to God just before I go to bed and just as I arise in the morning. I seem to hear Him best just before I get out of bed in the morning. It is quiet and I'm just starting to awake, and He speaks. Sometimes, He wants me to know He loves me. Sometimes He gives me insight into why certain people in my life are the way they are. He shows me who they are to Him. Other times, He gives me direction on how to be with someone in my life. I have heard him many times give me direct orders to talk to my children or my wife about certain things.

If you are reading this then I would venture to guess you've been chosen by God to see the needs of your family and friends and pray! Pray hard! Every day! For them and the releasing of strongholds that bind them! Then listen! Listen hard! Listen to God's direction. What is He calling you to do and be for the people in your life? No stronghold is released without God's intervention. You are not the one who brought your friend to understand their weaknesses, God did. You were simply chosen by Him to be the one who He uses to do His work.

For some of you, you may be thinking you're not good enough to pray for your friends, or you wonder if God really listens to your prayers. Think again. God said, "If my people who are called by my name will **humble** themselves and pray and seek my face, and turn from their wicked ways, then I will hear from heaven, and will forgive their sin and heal their land." (2 Chronicles 7:14 NIV) God didn't say, "If only the holy, righteous church leaders" or "those who are well versed in my word would humble themselves and pray..." No, he said, "If my people who are called by my name will humble themselves and pray..." If you call yourself a Christian, if you have given your life to Jesus, you are called by His name, and are qualified to call upon Him to overcome any circumstance in your life and to intercede for those He has placed on your heart.

So, pray. Sink into His presence. It is for you to come closer to Him, which is what He desires every moment of every day.

What do I pray for?

So, you've decided to sit down and start praying for a friend. What do you pray for? It's simple—whatever your friend's needs are. This is where the value of a journal becomes handy. Writing down what's going on in their world will help you know what to pray for. By journaling your relationships, you are better able to keep track of what is important to them. Then pray for these things. Maybe it's the need of a new car, like our friend Kyle. Maybe it goes much deeper than that and is a need to overcome feelings of guilt, shame, anger, and bitterness from a prior rape. As your relationship grows, so will the needs of prayer. More layers of intimacy will be stripped away and with it you'll see more pain, discomfort, and suffering which will result in the need for more prayer.

Informed Intercession

In Francis Frangipane's book titled *The Three Battlegrounds*, he speaks of Satan's domain as a realm of darkness that works its way into the Mind, the Church, and geographical areas of land. He begins chapter one explaining, "Wherever there is darkness, the Devil will be." Is it too much of a stretch to say that spiritual darkness has entered into your school?

The attack is huge. Words like "Inclusión" and "Entitlement" are being used to change the way you see the world. Just last week the federal government issued a letter to all public schools stating the schools had to allow students to choose which bathroom they want to use or lose federal funding. This is a simple act of what is called moral relativism.

Moral relativism allows students in your school to be who they want to be and no one has the right to tell them differently. If I am a boy, and I want to use the girl's bathroom, then I have that right because it "feels" right for me to use the girl's bathroom. If anyone objects to my "entitlement," they should be punished for not allowing me to be who I am. How dare they! Does this sound familiar? Simply stated, moral relativism is a strategy of Satan to degrade the morality of our land—to pull us away from God's laws or true morality and live lawlessly.

Since the first day you stepped into Kindergarten, you've been told you have no right to an objectifiable opinion of any kind because it judges others and who are you to judge. It has left us with a generation unwilling to stand for what is morally right. The other day, I heard a reporter ask students who attend Columbia University in New York if they felt female mutilation was wrong. Everyone said they had no opinion. If a woman wanted to do that to her body, then she had that right. How would you have responded to this question? What if the question were directed toward pets? I'd venture to guess the students of Columbia University would have boldly stated it was wrong. Why? Because students have been indoctrinated to believe the harming of animals is wrong.

You and your school are in the thick of it as we've seen this thing called moral relativism soar to all-time heights. Satan's strategy is working. He knows that a morally relative society has no room for God. God and his moral code becomes rigid and no fun. To those that don't know God, they see religion as a way to control the people. To take their freedom away. This is why although every other lifestyle is being celebrated, Christianity is not. Satan has done an incredible job to silence you and your religion. Right now, it is speculated that only two percent of the students at your school are Evangelical Christians.

In the year 2000, I was involved with a ministry called Young Life. If you don't know, Young Life is an outreach ministry where adults befriend high school students to win their hearts over to Christ and in the process, have a lot of fun. I was assigned a high school in east San Diego called Valhalla High. Valhalla was a typical suburban high school that prided itself on academics. Each Wednesday during lunch break, the Christian Club would meet in a room to listen to a guest speaker. I'd always show up to hang with some of the students involved with Young Life.

One day, the student leader of the group told us we didn't have a speaker that day. Instead, we were going to go out to the courtyard (where the students ate lunch) to sing worship songs. When we left the room, there were about 40 students. By the time we had reached the courtyard, our group of dedicated evangelical Christians had grown to 20. We sang with love in our hearts as the persecution fell upon us in the form of grapes, cookies, and other lunch bag items being tossed in our direction. When I left Valhalla that day, God spoke to me. He said, "This is where the battle is. This is where Satan has waged his war on your land." When you walk the halls of your school, do you sense the darkness? If you were to take your fellow student Christian Club members out to your "courtyard," how many would follow?

Did you know you can call upon God at any time to commission His angels in and around your school (Hebrews 1:13-14; Psalm 91:11)? In other words, God has given you and me the power to pray for angels in the heavenly realm to come down upon us for protection. God gives you the Holy Spirit to discern what is going on spiritually in your world. If we sense spiritual oppression going on, it would make perfect sense for us to call on these angelic beings for protection or to war against the forces of evil.

Now let's go a little deeper in this thought. The devil and his followers were once angelic beings worshiping God in the heavenly realm. Because of their allegiance to the devil, these angelic beings were tossed from heaven along with the devil to fall upon the earth (Revelation 12:4–9). They too are designed by God to listen and respond to the hearts of men. People who call upon demons perform witchcraft and cast spells upon others. Those who read tarot cards call upon demons. Simply put, it is in the hearts of people that influence how these forces of good and evil play out in the heavenly realm.

According to George Otis Jr. in his book titled *Informed Intercession*, the only way one can intercede for his family, friends, and community is to know where and how demonic influences have established what are called territorial strongholds in his community over time. This takes hours of investigative research usually done in a library digging up archived articles that may lead the intercessor to understand how/why demonic influences have made their way into his community. Mr. Otis suggests to those who want to intercede on behalf of their community to actually map out where the forces of Good and evil are. This takes a lot of time and commitment to interview and discover how these territorial strongholds have established themselves. Once the homework has been done, it allows those who understand the power of prayer to pray against these strongholds. Mr. Otis has documented hundreds of "Awakenings" as God has moved against the forces of evil in towns throughout the world. It is truly amazing to see God move after hearing the cry of His people and it will absolutely grow your faith if you're ever a part of such an awakening.

If you have a heart for your school and see the spiritual forces of darkness dwelling over it, please visit www.theg2c.com/prayer to learn how you can become a prayer warrior for your school. The G2C website gives you step-by-step instructions to war against the spiritual darkness that impacts your school. It also gives you helpful info on how to pray for your friends and family.

We have come to the end of part one of this book. If you remember in Chapter One, I wrote of how Satan has been working since the 1960s to remove God from our culture. You are the final generation and the most pivotal one in Satan's scheme. In Chapter Two, I wrote of the lies Satan buries deep within our subconscious called strongholds. In Chapter Three, you learned of how these strongholds attach to different personalities. By understanding a person's personality, it can help us understand the stronghold Satan has on their mind. In Chapter Four, we saw real examples of how Jesus exposed these strongholds with the truth. He showed us how we could do the same. In Chapter Five, we learned of the steps of intimacy and how to go from knowing someone to calling them a brother or sister. In Chapter Six, we took a long hard look on how to love someone the way Jesus would. Finally, in this chapter, we learned of the greatest tool God has given us to bring Satan and his scheme tumbling down. It is the power of prayer and if used diligently, it could literally transform a nation. Wouldn't that be the coolest thing?

What if instead of only 2% of the students in your school being Evangelical Christians, it was the other way around? What if 98% of students in your school were Evangelical Christians? What if 98% of the students across America were Evangelical Christians? What would your school look like? What would your country look like (See Notables next page)? In the next part of this book, we are going to learn how to do just that given the tools we've learned of in part one of this book. Are you ready to take back God's land and squash Satan in the process? Are you ready to have meaningful relationships with friends in your school without wearing masks? If so, get with your mentor and talk about what your school would be like if everyone were a true Christian.

This next challenge is probably the biggest and most strenuous. It requires a lot of energy and prayer. Good luck, and you know the deal; may the Force be with you.

NOTABLES:

An Evangelical Christian is one who believes the tenants of the Bible to be true, is known to carry a Biblical Worldview, and is willing to express his/her views openly. In a blog post by Lisa Becker titled, *Sending Christian Children to Public Schools: What the Results Show*, reveals a chart from the Nehemiah Institute that illustrates as of 2015, only 4% of High School students have a Biblical Worldview. This Worldview is down from 38% in 1988. The Nehemiah Institute has designed a PEERS test which "consists of a series of statements carefully structured to identify a person's worldview."

In his book titled, *The Jesus Survey*, Mike Nappa reveals startling results of what teens say Jesus is and what He means to their lives. Looking at four distinct areas or tenants of faith (The Bible is trustworthy in what it says about Jesus Christ, Jesus Christ is God, Jesus Christ was God Incarnate who physically lived, died and rose from the dead, and Jesus Christ is the only way to Heaven), results correlated with Thom and Jess Rainer's book, *The Millennials* that roughly 56% of teens with a Biblical Worldview shared their faith with a non-believer last month. The Jesus Survey was conducted in the Summer of 2010. Taking both surveys into account, it can be estimated that only 2% of the students at your public High School will engage others about their faith.

To read these articles and or studies, please visit:

https://www.dayspringchristian.com/blog/christian-children-in-public-schools/

https://www.nehemiahinstitute.com/peers.php

https://youthministry.com/christian-teens-really-believe-jesus/

PART TWO — DOING

"These are the things you are to do: Speak the truth to each other, and render true and sound judgment in your courts; do not plot evil against your neighbor, and do not love to swear falsely. I hate all this," declares the LORD.

Zechariah 8:16-17 NIV

Do all things without grumbling or questioning, that you may be blameless and innocent, children of God without blemish in the midst of a crooked and twisted generation, among whom you shine as lights in the world, holding fast to the word of life, so that in the day of Christ I may be proud that I did not run in vain or labor in vain.

Philippians 2:14-16 ESV

8

GAME CHANGER

No man is worth his salt who is not ready at all times to risk his well-being, to risk his body, to risk his life in a great cause.

Theodore Roosevelt

People who do right, even when it's at a great cost, are the people who are remembered. It's easy to float along with the crowd; to be just kind of captured within the group. But when you stand up and do right, people will take notice.

Dr. David Jeremiah

In the year that King Uzziah died, I saw the Master sitting on a throne—high, exalted! — and the train of his robes filled the Temple. Angel-seraphs hovered above him, each with six wings. With two wings they covered their faces, with two their feet, and with two they flew. And they called back and forth one to the other,
Holy, Holy, Holy is GOD-of-the-Angel-Armies.
His bright glory fills the whole earth.
The foundations trembled at the sound of the angel voices, and then the whole house filled with smoke. I said,
"Doom! It's Doomsday!
I'm as good as dead!
Every word I've ever spoken is tainted—
blasphemous even!
And the people I live with talk the same way,
using words that corrupt and desecrate.
And here I've looked God in the face!
The King! GOD-of-the-Angel-Armies!"
Then one of the angel-seraphs flew to me. He held a live coal that he had taken with tongs from the altar. He touched my mouth with the coal and said,
"Look. This coal has touched your lips.
Gone your guilt,
your sins wiped out."
And then I heard the voice of the Master:
"Whom shall I send?
Who will go for us?"
I spoke up,
"I'll go.
Send me!"

Isaiah 6:1-8, The Message

Her name was Sarah and she was a student attending a small university in Minnesota. She worked at the mall to support herself through school. Even though she was miles away from home, living with roommates in a dorm, she was very close to her family. She did well in school and was studying to be an accountant. Needless to say, her parents were very proud of their daughter and they saw her doing the right things to have a bright future. All is good in the world of Sarah.

One summer, her church invited students to participate in a mission's trip to Uganda. The mission was to last two weeks and promised to be a life-changing event as the church would reach out to bring aid to the Ugandan refugees. Sarah, with the blessing of her mom and dad, decided to go.

When she arrived in Uganda, she couldn't believe the oppression these refugees were living in. I guess you could say God opened young Sarah's eyes and it hurt. Her compassion for these people grew quickly. Then Sarah heard something that sickened her soul.

There was an orphanage in town where the children were being sold by the government into sex slavery. Orphanages are the place children are taken to feel safe, yet in this case, they were anything but safe. They were being forced to have sex for food and a place to sleep. Worse, it was government officials orchestrating the abuse.

Sarah made what I call a God move in her life. She went to the US Embassy and requested help in shutting down this operation. They lent an ear and were sympathetic, but that was all. They told her there was nothing they could do. She didn't stop. With a couple of other missionaries, she went to the Ugandan government. Instead of pleading with them, she made demands. She told them she was a US citizen that would take this story to the world if they didn't stop abusing these children. She then moved into the orphanage to make sure the trafficking stopped. It did. Sarah called back home with her story. Her parents were so proud of her for standing up against the Ugandan government and winning.

Then Sarah made yet another God move. Prompted by a vision from the Lord, Sarah sensed the Ugandan government was appeasing her, and as soon as she left to come home, the trafficking and abuse would start again. So, she and a few others who shared the same heart of compassion, stayed in Uganda. What was to be a two-week summer mission turned into four, then eight. Her parents began to worry.

They pleaded with her to come home. Sarah refused. They told her she was making a bad move. She disagreed. As long as Sarah stayed, the horrific acts against these precious children stopped. God showed Sarah her value in the lives of these children and it was far more important than her life back home. Then Sarah made yet another God Move. She dropped out of school to take up permanent residence at the orphanage. That's right, she became a full-time missionary.

Her parents were beside themselves. To them Sarah was throwing away all that she had worked for. To Sarah, life began the day she landed in Uganda. It was full of adventure and purpose. It was full of relying on God and living for God. It was full of David vs. Goliath courage as she stood against the Ugandan government. She was a warrior princess for Jesus, and it was full.

Good Moves vs. God Moves

Society tells us what good moves are. Here are but a few: get an education, secure a professional job (doctor, lawyer, accountant, engineer), invest in the stock market starting at a young age, get married (this one may be changing), work for 40 years (building up your nest egg), buy a house, have children... You get the point. No doubt, these are all good moves. Sarah was on this path. Her parents were proud of her "good moves."

God moves, on the other hand, are full of risk that don't always look good on the surface. They require courage and faith (Galatians 2:20). Here are some big God moves: quit your full-time job, sell your house and move your family to a distant land to be a full-time missionary. Drop out of school to become a full-time missionary. Start a youth ministry after 20 years of being a Licensed Physical Therapist.

Not all God moves are big. There are smaller God moves like getting up in the morning a little early to read His word and journal what He is teaching you, standing up for a friend that is being bullied, speaking to a total stranger when you sense the prompting of God to start a conversation, spiritually mapping your school, praying over someone for healing or to release a friend from demonic influence, volunteering for outreach events in your community. These are all God moves. In summary, there are two criteria when making a God move: 1, hearing His call, and 2, obeying His command. He may ask you to do something unusual, odd, or simple. Regardless, when you hear Him calling, just do it, as the saying goes.

How Do I Know God is Speaking to Me?

My little girl is 10 years old and loves Jesus. She just has one problem—she doesn't hear Him speak to her. Like young Samuel in the Bible, she wants to hear His voice (1 Samuel 3). I keep telling her in time, she will hear Him. Until then, read the Bible and when a verse jumps out at you, journal what it (God) is saying to you. If you struggle to hear God's voice, I encourage you to do the same. At some point, like Samuel, you'll hear Him speak. Until then, the Bible is His written word. If a verse jumps out at you and leaves an impression on your heart, take notice. God is speaking to you.

How to Confirm It is The Voice of God and Not Satan

The simplest way to determine it is God speaking to you is to ask yourself, "Would Satan want me to do this or does it require faith in God to carry this out?" Let's say you hear God telling you to go up to a lonely student at your school and introduce yourself. Would Satan want you to do this? Of course not. Satan is all about isolation, so when you introduce yourself to someone feeling isolated, would this simple act require some measure of faith in God? Absolutely. This person may look up at you, call you a loser and tell you to leave him/her alone. You can bet you are being prompted by God.

Also, it is always a good idea to look into God's word to see if what you heard is being supported by God's word. He is the same yesterday, today, and forever (Hebrews 13:8), meaning He wouldn't tell you something opposite of what His word says. Finally, if you are really struggling with not being certain it was God, talk to your mentor. He or she may be able to pray for you and hear a confirmation that this is something God wants you to do.

Mistaken for Jesus

In Mike Yaconelli's book *Messy Spirituality*, he writes of a man named Daryl who reluctantly makes a God move in his life. Here's what he wrote:

> Every month the youth group at River Road Church visited Holcomb Manor, a local nursing home, to hold church services for the residents. Daryl, a reluctant youth group volunteer, did not like nursing homes. For a long time, he had avoided the monthly services. But when a flu epidemic depleted the group of sponsors, Daryl agreed to help with the next month's service as long as he did not have to be a part of the program.

During the service, Daryl felt awkward and out of place. He leaned against the back wall, between two residents in wheelchairs. Just as the service finished and Daryl was thinking about a quick exit, someone grabbed his hand. Startled, he looked down and saw a very old, frail, and obviously lonely man in a wheelchair. What could Daryl do but hold the man's hand. The man's mouth hung open and his face held no expression. Daryl doubted whether he could hear or see anything.

As everyone began to leave, Daryl realized he didn't want to leave the old man. Daryl had been left too many times in his own life. Caught somewhat off-guard by his feelings, Daryl leaned over and whispered, "I'm ... uh ... sorry, I have to leave, but I'll be back. I promise." Without warning, the man squeezed Daryl's hand and then let go. As Daryl's eyes filled with tears, he grabbed his stuff and started to leave. Inexplicably, he heard himself say to the old man, "I love you," and he thought, *"Where did that come from? What's the matter with me?"*

Daryl returned the next month, and the month after that. Each time it was the same. Daryl would stand in back, Oliver would grab his hand, Daryl would say he had to leave, Oliver would squeeze his hand, and Daryl would say softly, "I love you Mr. Leak." (He had learned the name, of course.) As the months went on, about a week before the Holcomb Manor service, Daryl would find himself looking forward to visiting his aged friend.

On Daryl's sixth visit, the service started, but Oliver still hadn't been wheeled out. Daryl didn't feel too concerned at first, because it often took the nurses a long time to wheel everyone out. But halfway into the service, Daryl became alarmed. He went to the head nurse. "Um, I don't see Mr. Leak here today. Is he okay?" The nurse asked Daryl to follow her and took him to room 27.

Oliver lay in his bed, his eyes closed, his breathing uneven. At forty years of age, Daryl had never seen someone dying, but he knew Oliver was near death. Slowly, he walked to the side of the bed and grabbed Oliver's hand.

When Oliver didn't respond, tears filled Daryl's eyes. He knew he might never see Oliver alive again. He had so much he wanted to say, but the words wouldn't come out. He stayed with Oliver for about an hour, then the youth director gently interrupted to say they were leaving.

Daryl stood and squeezed Mr. Leak's hand for the last time, "I'm sorry Oliver, I have to go. I love you." As he unclasped his hand, he felt a squeeze. Mr. Leak had responded!

He had squeezed Daryl's hand! The tears were unstoppable now, and Daryl stumbled toward the door trying to regain his composure.

A young woman was standing at the door, and Daryl almost bumped into her. "I'm sorry," he said, "I didn't see you."

"It's all right, I've been waiting to see you," she said. "I'm Oliver's granddaughter. He's dying, you know."

"Yes, I know."

"I wanted to meet you, she said. When the doctors said he was dying, I came immediately. We've always been very close. They say he couldn't talk, but he's been talking to me. Not much, but I know what he is saying. Last night he woke up. His eyes were bright and alert. He looked straight into my eyes and said, 'Please say good-bye to Jesus for me.' And he laid back down and closed his eyes.

"He caught me off guard and as soon as I gathered my composure, I whispered to him, 'Grandpa, I don't need to say good-bye to Jesus; you are going to be with Him soon, and you can tell Him Hello.'

"Grandpa struggled to open his eyes again. This time his face lit up with a mischievous smile, and he said as clearly as I'm talking to you, 'I know, but Jesus comes to see me every month and he might not know I've gone.' He closed his eyes and he hasn't spoken since."

"I told the nurse what he had said and she told me about you coming every month, holding grandpa's hand. I wanted to thank you for him, for me ... and, well, I never thought of Jesus as being as chubby and bald as you, but I imagine Jesus is very glad to have had you to be mistaken for him. I know Grandpa is. Thank you."

She leaned over and kissed Daryl on the forehead.

Oliver Leak died peacefully the next morning. If a reluctant follower like Daryl can be mistaken for Jesus, maybe you and I can too.

All of us, in one way or another, have an influence over history. It is a gift from God. He gives us free will, and with it a chance to move the world toward or away from Him.

Andy Williams made a difference in the world one day. Instead of walking into his cafeteria and buying 15 classmates' lunch, he brought a gun to school, shot and killed two students and injured 13 others. The choice was his and so too it is yours. Truth be told, your everyday moves change the world whether you pay attention to them or not. The question is which direction will your choices take this world?

The answer to the question "Why are you here?" lies within this truth. You are here to make a difference either for the forces of Good or the forces of Evil. What it takes is a concerted effort to sit down and figure out how you are going to play this game called life. Edmund Burke once said, "The only thing necessary for the triumph of evil is for good men [or women] to do nothing." Are you going to be a servant of the one true God and make some serious God moves? Or, are you going to stand idly by watching evil triumph? It really is up to you.

We started this chapter learning of a girl who decided to lay down her life for her God. This chapter was written so you could understand how important you are to God and Satan. When God gave you the freedom to choose, He took a great risk in you not choosing Him. Whether you are aware of it or not, you are making decisions that influence history every day. Small, seemingly insignificant decisions amount to what is now called your life. Remember, one of Satan's biggest strategies is to busy your schedule with things like school, homework, sports, band, club, youth group, chores, work, etc. The list goes on and on. I encourage you right now to bow your head and ask your God, if you weren't so busy doing life, what would He want you to do?

Once again, it is time to close this book and get with your mentor. He or she may have yet another challenge. As you can tell, they are getting progressively harder, so be prepared. May the Force be with you.

NOTABLES:

If you are thinking God has called you to be a lifelong missionary like Sarah, that is great. You can be just like her when you reach 18 years of age. Until then, you cannot make these decisions without your parents' consent. So please realize Sarah's story was to illustrate a huge God Move.

On Monday, March 5, 2001, at 9:20 a.m., a 15-year-old boy named Charles Andrew Williams pulled a .22-caliber revolver and began shooting at his high school in Santee, California. He killed two boys and injured 13 others. On June 20, 2002, Williams pled guilty to all accounts and was sentenced to 50 years in prison. On March 1, 2004, he was transferred to an adult prison. He is currently incarcerated at Calipatria State Prison.

In her book *Smart Money Smart Kids*, Rachel Cruze tells a story of an engaged couple attending a small private university who were sold out for Jesus. Their plan was to graduate from this small private university, get married, and enter the mission field.

There was just one problem. In their endeavor to make what society says are good moves and get a college degree, they racked up $80,000 worth in student loans each! With a typical job, this would take at least 20 years to pay off. What? That's right, they were going to enter a marriage with a combined debt of $160,000. Ms. Cruze told them they had no chance of going into the mission field with that kind of debt. Their dreams were shattered. Even if they wanted to make a God move, they simply could not because of the bondage they were in. God's word says, "The rich rule over the poor, and the borrower is slave to the lender." (Proverbs 22:7) So what may seem to society as a "good move" might just be a ploy of the devil to take you out of the game before you even get in.

9

THE G2C

Our deepest fear is not that we are inadequate. Our deepest fear is that we are powerful beyond measure. It is our light, not our darkness that frightens us most. We ask ourselves, 'Who am I to be brilliant, gorgeous, talented, and famous?' Actually, who are you not to be? You are a child of God. Your playing small does not serve the world. There is nothing enlightened about shrinking so that people won't feel insecure around you. We were born to make manifest the glory of God that is within us. It's not just in some of us; it's in all of us. And when we let our own light shine, we unconsciously give other people permission to do the same. As we are liberated from our own fear, our presence automatically liberates others.

Maryanne Williamson
(Used by Nelson Mandela in his 1994 Inauguration Speech)

You just gotta ignite the light
And let it shine
Just own the night
Like the Fourth of July
Cause baby you're a firework

Katy Perry, *Firework*

You know, sometimes all you need is twenty seconds of insane courage. Just literally twenty seconds of just embarrassing bravery. And I promise you, something great will come of it.

Benjamin Mee, *We Bought a Zoo*

For the LORD shall build up Zion;
He shall appear in His glory.
He shall regard the prayer of the destitute,
And shall not despise their prayer.
This will be written for **the generation to come**,
That a people yet to be created may praise the LORD.
For He looked down from the height of His sanctuary;
From heaven the LORD viewed the earth,
To hear the groaning of the prisoner,
To release those appointed to death,
To declare the name of the LORD in Zion,
And His praise in Jerusalem

Psalm 102:16-21

According to Winkie Pratney in his book entitled *Fire on the Horizon*, you have been written off as the biggest bunch of loser's contemporary society has ever seen. But the labeling doesn't stop there. Other words to describe your generation are unambitious, disconnected, uneducated (not your fault), unwilling to conform, and entitled. Winkie writes, "They've grown up in a world on the edge of a social safety-net collapse, doomed to holding down a McJob and living with their parents forever. But remember the story of the Ugly Duckling. Some fairy tales do come true."

If you look throughout Revival history, you see a similar theme: a nation who once followed God now turns away from Him, resultant oppression sets in as society reaps what it sows (Galatians 6:7). Then a select few, chosen by God (who society has written off), begin to stand boldly for Him. This boldness begins a visitation of the Holy Spirit and a thing called revival starts to form. Isn't it interesting in His-story, God chooses to use the rejects of society to lead His revivals? Years later, when we look back at these men and women, we see them as strong, courageous, and intentional, willing to step out of the norm to see the greater good of their society and men. We see them as heroes, the way God saw them all along.

Winkie describes two things God does when He decides to get His hands on who society votes least likely to succeed. First, He establishes a testimony. People like you and I who are willing to make God moves begin to capture the hearts and attention of others. A simple glance in the Bible and you see them everywhere. Who was Gideon to stand against the Midianites, or Moses to stand against Pharaoh? Who was David to stand against Goliath, or Daniel to stand against Nebuchadnezzar? Answer, all were willing to be used by God.

This testimony is usually started by two or three people who are willing to get on their knees and pray every day for a visitation of the

Holy Spirit. Other believers start to see what is happening and join in. Soon a spiritual war begins as these believers call for God to return their land to Him. Angels begin to war against demons in the spiritual realm. The darkness of immorality becomes fragmented and pierced.

The second thing God does to revive a land is He appoints a law. Once God has established a testimony, He will then turn back the *moral compass* to Him. Morality is a sign that people are living their lives in obedience to God's written Word. Immorality is the sign of a people, group, or nation acting in defiance to God. When a nation who once knew God turns from Him, they stop following His laws. They then make up their own laws. This usually is followed by God's hand of provision being lifted from them. The result is a nation who suffers from what it has sown. A simple test to determine if a person, family, community, county, state, or nation is following God is to see if they are living by His precepts (laws). In a land where anything is accepted, and everything goes, the people lose sight of what is right from what is wrong. We are now living in that time. All you have to do is look at the Supreme Court of America to see what society dictates as right from wrong. In the last 50 years they have taken prayer and God out of schools, removed all God artifacts from government property, allowed mothers to kill their own babies, and legislated the legal right for same sex marriage. (I could keep going, but I think you get the point.) All lead to immorality and all are in direct defiance of God's Word or laws (Romans 1:16-32).

We all have a moral compass. We all inherently know what is right and good and what is wrong and evil. Things like murder, rape, and stealing are wrong no matter what society you live in. Have you ever done something that was stupid? What told you it was stupid? Just as rocks are hard, water is wet, and fire is hot, so too are God's moral laws well defined. Seriously, can you take the life of another and feel no shame even if your government says it's legal?

Giving and Taking

Right and wrong is really about giving and taking. Just look at all the laws of the Bible and you will see this theme played out. The intent behind what is right and good is giving. When we give to give, we express our love toward God and others. When we give to get, well that's another story. Manipulation does not go well with God's moral laws. We could easily replace *give to get* with *give to take*. Then there is flat out taking. It is pretty evident this is not morally acceptable. So, when God establishes His law, what is really happening is the people are acknowledging the moral law of the Bible to be right and inherently good. They understand the love of a Father wanting them to live life the way He intended, so they follow Him and His law.

Revival starts with a few standing to give to others in a way that shows the love of Christ. A few grow to a few more, which grows to a group, then a community, and finally a nation. It requires a special generation hard wired by God to carry out such a task. I'd like to once again refer to Winkie Pratney in his book *Fire on the Horizon* as he has so eloquently described who you are in the eyes of God. He uses a prophetic scripture in Psalms that points to you and your generation when unwrapped in its original language.

For he established a testimony in Jacob and appointed a law in Israel, which he commanded our fathers, that they should make them known to their children:

That in their last revolution of time the (slacker) generation to come (from out of the west) might know (by actually seeing) the children (nation, family to come) which shall be born who shall rise to accomplish, (make good, make their mark, celebrate) and declare [them] in turn to their children. That they might set their hope in (the supreme and greatest just)

God, and not forget the works of (this Almighty powerful) God, but keep his commandments.

And might not be as their fathers, a stubborn and rebellious generation; a generation that set not their heart aright, (would not stand up at the center for anything) and whose spirit is not steadfast with God's. The children of Ephraim, being armed (equipped with weapons), and carrying bows, turned back (became perversely converted back) in the day of battle.

They kept not (did not guard, build a hedge about) the covenant of God and utterly refused to walk in His Law. And forgot (became oblivious by not paying attention to) His works, (thoroughly effecting exploits) and His wonders (distinctive marvels & miracles) that He had showed them.

Psalms 78:5-11, *Expanded Hebrew Version*

Psalms 78 speaks of a "generation to come" and reveals a background to their birth. It speaks of God's dealings with their parents before them, of a great divine visitation marked by wonders and miracles. The visitation was not just for blessing; it was to give them courage and faith for a great battle to come upon them in the near future.

These parents were given both short range and long-range weaponry to prepare them for the battle at hand and a greater one still beyond that. Yet on the very eve of the battle, just when it counted most, they forgot their covenant with God, forgot what He had done and what He said, forgot both His works and His wonders. They abandoned their call, folded their tents and their hearts and left their children to face the war alone.

There have been many generations in history that might claim for themselves the promise in this passage, who likewise found themselves in the situation described in Psalms 78. You are not the only ones in history that might claim it, but you most certainly fit the spirit and intention of God's protective visitation.

While historical records in Scripture are rarely subject to interpretation, prophetic phrases certainly are, as we try to determine from a past declaration a future intention of God. This is tricky in an original language, let alone in a translation. God speaks to people about what He intends to do beyond what they can possibly see, and we know that because of the nature of such revelation, prophets often recorded what they did not understand.

Who are the people described in the prophetic psalm? They are simply called "the generation to come." The phrase is not common, only used this way twice in the Bible. The word "generation" means a revolution of time, another whole cycle of history.

Winkie Pratney, *Fire on the Horizon*

Some have described Winkie as a modern-day prophet. When he wrote *Fire on the Horizon* in 1998, he could see, like us all, the world's movement away from the moral code of God. He could also see, unlike us all, a generation of youth groomed by God to stop the intent of corruption on our land. When he wrote these words, he referred to the "generation to come" as the *slacker generation*. This generation appeared to be that of the Gen-X ers, a small group of kids born between 1965 and 1979. Now, some years later, it appears the generation Winkie prophetically spoke of is more appropriate for the 78 million millennials and Gen-Z ers in the world today.

Interestingly, Winkie goes on to dissect the words *generation* and *to come* in their original Hebrew language. The word *generation* in this prophetic passage means to hold off, hinder, or tarry. The words *to come* literally means *last* with its root word translated *facing eastward, i.e., western*. So, this prophetic "generation to come" literally means a last generation of youth coming out of the west who are in no hurry to grow up. Instead, they appear to be hard wired by God to turn their hearts back to Him and not the immorality of their forefathers.

Is Pastor Winkie right? Could there be a generation of youth coming out of the west with a conviction so strong they could stand against the principalities of Satan in their land? If so, how old would this band of youth be? Are they middle school kids? High school kids? Or would young adults in college be who God calls? Which do you think is best equipped to lead this movement? To get our answer, we may have to look to science and more specifically how the brain develops to see who may be best equipped to stand against Satan in our land.

How Your Brain Develops

Research shows that neural or nerve development of the brain continues well into young adulthood (See Notables for reference). Recently, science has discovered that this development occurs in waves. Likewise, different areas of the brain grow at different rates. During pre-adolescence, the prefrontal cortex, located just behind one's forehead, is growing at an alarming rate, while the cerebellum, located at the base of one's skull just above the neck, shows little growth. Just three to four years later, growth of the prefrontal cortex slows way down, as the growth of the cerebellum speeds up.

The prefrontal cortex is described as the part of the brain that reasons. As a matter of fact, it is known as *the area of sober second thought*. This is where most abstract learning takes place.

It would seem logical then to think that periods of growth would result in increased learning, but it does not. In fact, the opposite occurs. It is not *neurons* that create thought but in fact *neural pathways* that create the ability to reason and comprehend. Your ability to add two plus two together is the firing of an electrical impulse down a series of nerves called a neural pathway. The more times this pathway is fired upon, the deeper the comprehension becomes. When the brain begins to develop many new neurons during a growth period, few are associated with pathways. These new neurons have yet to develop into "burned" pathways. There is greater chance a nerve impulse will fire down the wrong path making comprehension and reasoning difficult.

The cerebellum has a different function. It has always been associated with physical coordination, but recently science has discovered cerebellar activity when the brain is processing mental tasks. Dr. Jay Giedd, a neuroscientist from the National Institute of Mental Health, explained the complex actions of the cerebellum this way. "It's like a math co-processor. It's not essential for any activity... but it makes any activity better. Anything we can think of as higher thought— mathematics, music, philosophy, decision-making, social skill—draws upon the cerebellum. To navigate the complicated social life of the teen and to get through these things instead of lurching seems to be a function of the cerebellum."

Whereas increased growth of the prefrontal cortex worsens reasoning, increased growth of the cerebellum improves it. Since the cerebellum doesn't significantly grow until high school age, it would make sense why middle school kids seem so much more uncoordinated physically as well as in reasoning.

Now let's try to bring this back to the issue of who is better equipped to deliver revival to our land. Many youth pastors would agree that there is a phase in a young evangelical Christian's walk where they begin to wake up to the faith they are practicing. This awakening usually comes with much thought and introspection. Whereas they once adopted the faith of their parents, they begin to wonder if this is something they really want for themselves. You may have been there or may be there now. If you are, don't worry, this is exactly where God wants you. Your brain has developed to the point where you are now able to really understand the message of Christ, and more importantly, your salvation.

Many middle schoolers are very much socially dependent upon their parents' faith. Family and friends are at the center of their life. And, because their brain has yet to fully mature, they struggle to see beyond themselves and their circumstances. They also have yet to really test their faith and claim it as their own.

A high school student, on the other hand, has matured to the point where they can see beyond themselves, their family and friends. Neural pathways are developed, reasoning begins to take shape, and they are ready to claim their faith. They have the capacity to see beyond themselves and into their friends' lives. Simply put, they have the ability to cry for another.

Unfortunately, life and society seem to speed up when a student reaches high school. He or she is now being impressed by society to consider what college to attend, what degree to attain, and what career to chase. Days are filled with activity, but not nearly so full as that of the university student.

Young adults in the university setting are subject to so much interference on their faith. They are constantly bombarded with distraction. Although many high school students are confronted with sex, drugs, and rock 'n roll, college students are inundated with it. I've heard so many testimonies from both young and old, who described themselves to be *out of control* in college. Later, as a follower of Christ, they resent those "rebellious" years. The attack Satan has on those (especially Christians) is downright mind blowing. In the university setting, so many students are faced daily with decisions to follow Christ or Satan. There really is no room in between.

There is no one better suited to carry out this one last revival on our land than you. You have the energy, the courage, and the focus needed to hear from God and make serious God moves for Him. Now please don't misunderstand me, God can use anyone He pleases. If he wants middle schoolers to lead a revival in our land, then that is what will happen. If he chooses to use college-aged young adults to lead revival in our land, then so be it. My point is simple. You have the ability to move your school, city, and nation toward Him.

"But how can I create revival?" you ask. "I'm only one person. I'm shunned at school for my faith. How am I going to get my school let alone my city to follow Christ?" Simple, you take the moral high ground.

In this chapter, we learned of a generation that will carry one last revival before Jesus returns. A revival that will start in the west and move eastward. They are a generation of youth that appear to the world as a bunch of disconnected, unambitious losers. God, however, sees them much differently. He has created them for this time in world history. They have a hunger to worship their God and by doing so shine God's love to the rest of the world. It appears you have been chosen and in this next chapter, we are going to learn how God is going to use you and other dedicated Christians to turn this country back to Him.

Now meet up with your mentor to talk about what you learned in this chapter. He or she may have another challenge for you. Be prepared and may the Force be with you.

QUOTABLES:

Don't sell yourself short trying to live in the moment. Fireworks come and go.

When it all fades away like seasons do tell me, what will you have to show?

Cause you are not some cosmic accident. You are wonderfully made.

And here's a digit for being you so you could live this way.

We gotta shine, shine, shine like the stars in the sky

And we gotta live, live, live like we're willing to die.

We gotta open up and love enough to show that we are more than meets the eye.

Micah Tyler, *More Than Meets the Eye*

NOTABLES:

The story of *The Ugly Duckling*

https://www.youtube.com/watch?v=qafXdmFsTbE

For a thorough reference of neural development of the brain, read:

Principles of Neural Science, Fifth Edition by Eric R. Kandel, James H. Schwartz, et al. Part VIII Development and the Emergence of Behavior.

Also see *Adolescent Brains Are Works in Progress* by Sarah Spinks

https://www.pbs.org/wgbh/pages/frontline/shows/teenbrain/work/adolescent.html

10

TAKING THE MORAL HIGH GROUND

As I fumble with the gift of my free will
He says hush now, listen to my voice, be still
My refuge, my Father
The only Living Water
I'm weary, I'm broken
I've cracked my heart wide open
Unholy, unworthy
And still You reassure me
You knew me
Before I knew myself
I don't wanna be, I don't wanna be lost again

Saving Jane, *Grace*

Flo: "What's he up to, Doc?"
Doc: "What are you doing, Kid?"
Lightning: "I think the King should finish his last race."
Doc: "You just gave up the Piston Cup. You know that?"
Lightning: "Ah, this grumpy old race car I know once told me something. 'It's just an empty cup.'"

Cars, 2006; Pixar/Disney Motion Pictures

He who saves a life, saves the world in time.

Jewish Proverb

On May 3, 1980, a 13-year-old girl named Cari Lightner was struck and killed by a hit and run driver while walking to a church carnival in Fair Oaks, California. Police notified her mother, Candace Lightner, of the horrific accident, but they failed to tell her the driver was drunk and just two days out on bail from another drunk driving hit and run. It was his fifth drunk driving offense in four years. Candace found out this terrible truth when she drove down to the site of the accident and spoke with some of the police officers. Candace Lightner was outraged. She no longer had the gift of her daughter because of some repeat offender the system wasn't equipped to handle.

Candace began doing some research and found that alcohol was involved in some 60% of all fatal car crashes. This amounted to thousands of children dying at the hands of drunk drivers every year. So, Candace made a "God move" in her life and decided to fight until the system changed.

She formed an organization called Mothers Against Drunk Drivers (MADD) and began soliciting mothers all over the country for their support. MADD began as a rebellion against the system that indirectly supported an act that seemed morally wrong to anyone willing to listen. Within months, MADD had convinced the governor of California to form a committee that would investigate the prevalence of this problem. Candace, heading up this committee, quickly convinced politicians something had to be done. Within months, laws were passed to help law enforcement fight against drunk driving, not only at the state level, but at the federal level as well.

MADD had become a massive social movement that continues to grow to this day. Interestingly, there have been many social movements that start with a spark, seem to gain momentum, then suddenly die out. What did MADD do that these other organizations failed to do? The answer is simple, MADD decided to reach for "The Moral High Ground". The moral high ground comes when you stand for something or someone no one else can stand against.

Instead of focusing their attention and criticism on drunk driving, MADD decided to focus on the protection and well-being of children. They turned vehicular manslaughter of a child into a moral issue everyone could identify with. They decided to preach the need to keep children safe, and what better way than to impose stricter laws on those who kill a child while intoxicated. They identified a morality in an area never explored. More importantly, their moral message could not be opposed. Who in their right mind would oppose a group of mothers wanting stricter laws passed to protect the safety and well-being of their children?

MADD to this day continues to be a strong, vibrant movement fighting for the same thing it fought for in 1980. We can learn a great deal from how MADD took the moral high ground and how God wants to take back His land in much the same way.

Who or What Are You Crying for?

There is an interesting thing about tears; they tell a person a lot
about themselves. Tears only come in two forms—for yourself or for
others. When we shed tears for ourselves, it is usually in the form of
pity and discontent. Do you have a friend in your life who never seems
happy, always complaining, always feeling they are being taken
advantage of? Who would you say they are crying for? On the other
hand, do you have a friend always thinking about others in need,
wanting to do something to help, saddened that these people are
hurting? Simply put, victims shed tears for themselves while victors
shed tears for others.

To contrast MADD and their moral movement, let's look at a
movement that, much like MADD, was an overnight success, but unlike
MADD could not sustain itself. The movement I'm referring to is the
Freedom Movement of the 1960s. It was authored by young teenage
baby boomers who lived by the mantra, "If it feels good, do it." To a
point, an awakening in America was happening but only in a self-
serving way. Within roughly 10 years, this movement began to
crumble. The reason was simple—they lacked tears for another.

MADD has been crying for children since their inception. They have
been crying for the countless victims whose lives ended short because
of the immoral recklessness of another. If you were to visit MADD's
web site, you'll see countless pictures of young girls and boys whose
lives have been taken. Run your pointer over a pic and you get a short
bio of the child and their tragic death. You can't help but cry for these
true victims. (www.madd.org) As long as there are people whose lives
have been struck short by reckless drunk driving, there will be MADD.

**Christianity moves when those touched by God begin to cry
for another.** This is what happened to Sarah when visiting Uganda.
The same happened to Daryl when he visited Mr. Leak at Holcomb

Manor. If you are concerned for your friends and willing to make God moves, you will shake the earth you walk on. Victory, my friend, is in the tears.

Are You Ready to Cry for Your Friends?

> She says, "It's only in my head."
> She says, "Shh, I know it's only in my head."
> But the girl on the car in the parking lot
> Says: "Man, you should try to take a shot
> Can't you see my walls are crumbling."
> Then she looks up at the building
> And says she's thinking of jumping.
> She says she's tired of life;
> She must be tired of something.
>
> Counting Crows, *Round Here*

> When you feel you've had enough and you've wasted all you love, I'll be here for you, here for you
>
> Kygo, *Here for You* (Feat Ella Henderson)

In 2001, President George W. Bush decided it would be best for our educational system to impose No Child Left Behind. This was the government's way of saying, "Too many children are flunking out of school." So, laws were passed to keep children moving along within the system whether they learned or not.

God, on the other hand, has a different reason to leave no child behind. As Christians, God is calling us to stand for those in our schools who don't feel loved, appreciated, or included. The woman at the well was one such person. Jesus' intent that day was simple. He wanted her to know that despite her flaws, He loved her just the way she was. I believe, every person young or old should feel the love of another just the way they are. To feel accepted and approved of. To be included and welcomed. You should, I should, everyone should.

Unfortunately, students today feel rejected and excluded by their peers. If you feel this way, you are not alone. No one seems to feel they measure up. Teenage suicide rates are at an all-time high. Satan's greatest deception is to convince a person he or she doesn't matter. No one cares. No one appreciates. No one takes notice. God on the other hand created us to first have relationship with Him, then have relationship with one another. Where Satan wants to isolate us from our fellow man, God wants us to embrace our fellow man. Even with the hope of Christ in our hearts, we can fall into depression. Imagine how much worse depression must be to those who don't have the hope of Christ in their heart?

What if you don't believe in Jesus or God like 98% of the students that go to your school? What if you were never taught of God's love? What if you learned in school that you evolved as a species from a primordial soup pot of single-celled organisms? The message is clear. Chance is the only reason you are here so don't think there is some deep meaning to your life. And certainly, don't believe there is someone out there who cares. After all, all of us are here by chance trying to find our own way.

Like MADD standing for the safety of children, revival will come upon our land when we as Christians cry for those who feel lost, lonely, and unloved. As soon as we do, we will be victors. We will take the moral high ground and God will take back his land. St. Francis of Assisi once said, "Always preach the word of God, when necessary use words." Remember, no one cares about how much you know until they know how much you care. Are you ready to start caring, to start crying for the lost, lonely, and unloved in your school? If yes, read on. If no, put this book down; it will be of no use to you.

> Jesus, undeterred, went right ahead and gave his charge. "God authorized and commanded me to commission you: Go out and train everyone you meet, far and near, in this way of life, marking them by baptism in the threefold name: Father, Son, and Holy Spirit. Then instruct them in the practice of all I have commanded you. I'll be with you as you do this, day after day, right up to the end of the age."
>
> Matthew 28:18-20 (MSG)

Jesus wasn't joking around when he commissioned his disciples. He knew He had finished his work and now it was man's turn to shine like Christ. When I read this verse, this is what I hear. "Go with courage to those who need Me in their heart. Love on them as I would. Show them who I am, not through your words, but through your actions. Take them under your wing and teach them all I have taught you. If you do this, your life will be full, and I will be with you to the end."

Your Final Challenge, If You Choose to Accept It.

Until now you've been receiving challenges from your mentor. I want to commend you for your effort. You have been a mighty force for the Lord in your community. These challenges were designed to help you realize that life becomes rewarding when serving another. And even though they got harder each week, you hung in there and made a difference. Now you'll receive one last challenge from me, and it will be by far the most challenging to carry out. Whereas you were challenged to do something through the week, now I encourage you to take this one last challenge for the school year. Like all the other challenges you've met over the last nine weeks, they are not difficult to understand yet require bold God moves to carry out.

When you go to school silently pray for God to show you three people (same sex as you) that you don't know. When you hear Him speak to you and say, "There. That person. I want you to start praying for that person." Then, I want you to commit to befriending that person as God directs you into their life. This person may be an underclassman, lonely, unusual in the way they dress, gay, lesbian, of another race, or maybe overwhelmingly popular. Like Jesus being intentional with the woman at the well, I ask that you be intentional in this person's life. "Hi my name is _____. What's yours?" is a great start.

Listen to God as he directs you into that person's life. Try to get a feel for their personality type and the strongholds of Satan you learned of in chapters two and three. Boldly move down the five steps of intimacy using the phenomenon of initiate/reciprocate you learned of in chapter five. Work hard to understand their primary love language you learned of in chapter six. Pray for this person daily as learned in chapter seven. Be intentional about tearing down the strongholds of unbelief in their mind. At any time in the process you need another to confide in, your mentor is there for you ready and willing.

Let me be clear, your role is not to befriend them so you can convert them to Christianity. If you love on them the way Jesus did, it will naturally come at the right time for them to start asking you questions. So please, don't introduce yourself saying, "Hi my name is _____. Do you know Jesus? What are you doing Wednesday night? Would you like to come to my church youth group?" Instead of talking about Jesus and your church, I want you to be Jesus in their life and love on them. Find common ground and work to understand their interests in life. If they like to shop, invite them to go shopping with you at the mall. If they like to fish, invite them to go fishing with you. If they like sports, invite them to a college or professional game.

Like all the other challenges you've faced this summer, this challenge isn't hard to understand. All you have to do is go out and love on three people the way Christ would without talking about Him, your church, or your religion. Instead, figure out their personality, pray against the strongholds that bind them. Figure out their love language. Speak into their heart against the strongholds in a language they understand. If they ask why you are doing this (if the stronghold is big enough in their life, they will wonder why you care), just tell them you admire them for _____ (fill in the blank) and you like being their friend. When you've stepped down the intimacy path and have permission to be a close friend, it's time to share your story. This may take a few months or even the whole school year, but in due time, you'll be able to share your faith when the soil of their heart is ripe to hear what you have to say (Matthew 13:1-23).

How to Share Your Story

If you looked me right in the eye
Would see the pain deep inside
Would you take the time to
Tell me what I need to hear
Tell me that I'm not forgotten
Show me there's a God
Who can be more than all I've ever wanted
'Cause right now I need a little hope
I need to know that I'm not alone
Maybe God is calling you tonight
To tell me something
That might save my life

Sidewalk Prophets, *Save My Life*

If you are a Christian, you have a story of how God sought you out, picked you up, cleaned you off, and placed a desire in your heart to see others do the same. It's called your testimony and it is the most powerful tool God has given you. Your story is impactful because it is how you met or came to know Jesus, and no one can argue against it. This will undoubtedly leave a mark with anyone who hears it. Before giving your testimony, you may want to throw out a teaser, "I met Jesus _____." This is stated to grab the attention of your friend or group of friends you are talking to. For myself, I met Jesus on a bus in New Zealand. Maybe you met Jesus at a camp. Where was the camp located? At a lake in the California Sierras, or maybe on the streets of Compton? Avoid stating the church group or name of the camp. In other words, instead of saying, "I met Jesus at a Young Life camp," say, "I met Jesus on a mountain in Colorado." Regardless, this is a great lead into your story.

A testimony generally has four parts to it. The first part is your background. This is where you paint the picture of your life with broad strokes. Depending upon how much time you have, you may want to talk about your mom and dad, siblings, and where you grew up. In this part of your testimony it is important to be real and talk about the stronghold Satan had on your life and some of the emotional pain you were dealing with at the time. Maybe you didn't feel good enough to be loved. Maybe you turned to drugs to mask the pain of your parents' divorce, or maybe you were contemplating suicide because life had gotten so bad. Likewise, this is the part of your testimony where you want to talk about how God was working in your life before you even knew Him. I call these God markers. I have a friend who was shot at when he was a teenager. The bullet missed his head by two inches. Even though he didn't give his life to Christ until years later, he believes this was a God marker in his life as he knows now God stopped that bullet from hitting him. Regardless, this is why you want to wait until you are a close friend before sharing your story.

The second part of your testimony is focused on the events that show how God started to steer you toward Him. Maybe it was someone who befriended you and stood by you as you dealt with your circumstances. Maybe it was a book you were reading that started to open your eyes to who Jesus was and who He could be for you. Or maybe it was a camp or event that you were invited to. Clearly talk about how doors opened up and made it possible for Him to meet you.

In the third part of your testimony, you want to talk about that moment Jesus came into your life. In this part of your testimony draw a picture of where you were and what was going on around you as you came to the reality you needed Jesus in your heart. Maybe you heard Him speak to you, or you felt this weight just fall off your shoulders as you cried out to Him. If you were like me, this part is usually hard to talk about without choking up. Realize your transparency is a good thing, especially when speaking to a close friend. The final part of this testimony is to explain how your life changed in that moment. Maybe the depression suddenly disappeared, or the addiction went away, or the void you had been feeling was suddenly gone. Make sure to touch upon this as this is the miracle in your life.

The fourth and final part of your testimony is an invitation. As a close friend, you know what your friend is dealing with. You know the stronghold Satan has on their life. You know their personality and you have the permission to speak into their heart. If the setting is intimate enough, it is time to let them know this and ask them if they are ready to have this Jesus rescue them from their stuff as well.

A wise Christian once said to me, "What good is your testimony if you don't follow it with an invitation?" This may be a time when a lot of questions come up. Don't be surprised if God starts speaking through you. Honestly, whatever you say to your friend in this moment is probably what God wants you to say. Also, if you go to www.theg2c.com/searching, we have put together a page that answers common questions a non-believer may have.

Finally, it is beneficial to have three versions of your testimony that are adjusted to the amount of time you have. I call this a short version (2-4 minutes); a medium version (10 – 20 minutes); and a long version (20 – 40 minutes). All should be in your hip pocket, ready to go in a moment's notice. If you go to www.theg2c.com/testimony, we've created a page where you can upload a 2-4-minute video of your short version. Giving your testimony in front of a camera is great practice. Likewise, having a web page full of testimonies is great for the world to see. Remember, your story is the most powerful witness God has given you. For purposes of illustration, I have written my short version of my testimony, so you can get a better understanding of what I mean.

I Met Jesus on a Bus in New Zealand

When I met Jesus on a bus in New Zealand, I was lonely and confused, thinking if I met the right girl, all my loneliness would go away. I was 29 and just finishing up ten years of college.

I decided to take a trip to New Zealand to clear my head. I had just had yet another break-up from a girl I thought I was going to marry. I decided to grab a book to read on the plane considering the 12-hour flight. It was called *When You Can't Come Back*, by Dave Dravecky.

Each chapter of the book described a season of time in Dave's life with his father. From the earliest of memories to when his father passed away. At the end of each chapter, Dave did an incredible job of paralleling the love of his biological father with the love of God our Heavenly Father. Being raised Catholic, I was taught that Jesus hung on the cross for the world, not for me. This was the first time I had ever seen God as someone who loved me and wanted to have a personal relationship with me.

On my last night there, I had to take an all-night bus ride from Wellington to Auckland where I was to catch a plane home the next day. The book was heavily on my mind. I really can't tell you why, but I decided to ask God a question, "God, you've always been there for me, haven't you?" In a soft voice that I heard in my head He said, "Yes, Brett, I have always been there for you." "And you'll always be there for me, won't You? I responded." In an even softer yet resolute voice He said, "Yes, Brett. I will always be there for you!" In that moment, I broke down and began to cry. For the first time in my life the loneliness was gone. The void of not having a companion in my life was gone.

You know _____ (name). I see you struggling with _____ (stronghold). I also know God loves you very much. He has a huge plan for your life, and it isn't believing in _____ (restate stronghold). But it takes you admitting you have scars on your soul only God can take away. That is why Jesus hung on a cross; to take away these scars known as sins. I also want you to know Satan is working overtime to keep you away from God. He is getting you to do this by creating doubt in your mind of who God is and how much He loves you. And that is the bottom line. He loves you just the way you are; scars and all. So, what do you say? Let's kick Satan and this _____ (stronghold) to the curb. Are you willing to take whatever faith you have in God right now and combine it with my faith and pray with me? Let's ask Jesus to come into your heart and take away this _____ (stronghold). I guarantee you will have a freedom you've never experienced before.

Babe

When I was 38, my grandfather, Albert Cummins, passed away. His memorial service took place in a small Catholic church near his home in Pine Grove, California. The funeral, however, was to be carried out some 100 miles away at Holy Cross Catholic Cemetery in South San Francisco. After the service, a large processional of cars followed the hearse as it made its way down from the gold country to the bay area. I was about to witness one of the most touching moments of my life.

Grumpa (this was his nickname) was to lie next to his wife Doris in a crypt for eternity. Just after the priest had spoken and before the crew lifted Grumpa's casket into the crypt, an old Lincoln Town Car pulled up to the site. A gentleman about Grumpa's age got out of the car and walked hurriedly toward us. He started asking if this was the site of Mr. Albert Cummins. His name was Babe and he was here to say goodbye to a lifelong friend.

He found familiar faces and began to realize he had just made it in time. He asked if he could have a moment with his old friend before the workers placed Al into the crypt. The workers backed off and gestured it would be fine. "Take your time," one of them said. So, Babe slowly made his way to the casket. He gently laid his hand on the casket and began to mumble something all the while tenderly rubbing the casket with his hand. Then he laid his cheek on the casket and began to cry. Understanding the sincerity of the moment, we all began to cry as well. He then lifted his head up, kissed the casket, wiped his tears away, and stepped back gesturing to the crew he was done.

As he backed away toward us, we couldn't help but ask him what he had said. He looked at us and said, "I've known Al for 65 years. He has been a lifelong friend. One day when we were young, he and I made a pact with each other. If one were to outlive the other, then we promised we'd be at the other's funeral to pay our last regards. I had planned on being here on time, but earlier this week I got double pneumonia and was admitted into the hospital. I kept thinking they were going to release me, but they didn't. So, early this morning, I checked myself out of the hospital and drove the two hours hoping I'd make it in time. All I said to him was how much I appreciated him and would never forget all the lifelong memories we had made together. I also told him I would miss him and hope someday we could be together again."

Babe died four months later.

Do you have a friend like this? Someone you've made a lifelong commitment to. What would it feel like to make a promise to someone that no matter what, if you lived longer than them, you'd be at their funeral to see them off?

Everyone needs a Babe in their life. You do. I do. The whole world does. So, I want you to seek out these three individuals with the intention of making the same lifelong commitment. I want you to see these newfound friends as friends for life. Sure, they are going to have their faults. So what? So do you. Any less of a commitment to them and this challenge will be lost.

I have three close friends that I have made this pact with. There are at least another 20 people in my life that if I outlive, I will be at their funeral. To be honest, this is pathetic. It should be more, and I'm working on it. I encourage you to not wait but start making this pact with those who matter most.

How A Lifelong Commitment Equals Revival

If you go to www.theg2c.com, you'll find tools that will help you walk the path with your newfound friends. I know, you are thinking,

"How can I pick out three friends and God create revival?" Let me show you what God showed me.

There are roughly 2% of the students in your school who are evangelical Christians. This means they are bold enough to stand for and share their faith. For the sake of simplicity, let's say you go to a high school of a hundred students and you are one of two evangelical Christians in your school. If each of you were to accept this challenge and befriend three students each with the intent to be a friend for life, by the end of the school year at least two of the three will become like a brother or sister in your life. It is then, you have the permission and responsibility to share your faith and invite them to pray the sinner's prayer with you. When they say yes, obviously your work isn't done. They need to get plugged in to your youth group, and you need to keep loving on them. Once plugged in, challenge them to read this book over the next summer.

By the next school year, there will be six students including you who now have accepted the challenge to love on three new students. Let's say again two out of the three come to know the love of Christ and choose to walk with Him. This will mean by year three, there will be 18 students ready to accept the challenge and find three lifelong friends of their own. This would amount to 54 students being loved on in the beginning of year three. Again, using the formula that two out of three will accept Christ by the end of the school year, then the original 18 plus 36 students (i.e. 54 students) will go into year four committed to make three lifelong friendships of their own. By the end of year four there won't be enough lifelong friends for each to find. This is called revival and God is ready. He just needs you to befriend three strangers this school year and selflessly love on them.

If you think this is going to be no fun, think again. Yes, you are committing with intention to making new friends and growing your relationship with them, but the upside for you is huge. You will have friends you can trust so you don't have to pretend you are someone you are not. Each year your circle of friendship will grow and so too your popularity as these people called your friends get that you care about each one. You'll be able to pray for these people and watch God work in their lives. You'll see incredible miracles as Satan's strongholds fall to God's truth. You'll be able to watch your friends grow in God as they begin to pray for others. Your school will be one where all kids will be respected and loved while still celebrating each's unique qualities of who God called them to be. Being part of a movement like this is fun, exciting, and full of purpose. As St. Irenaeus once said, "God's love is man fully alive." Life will matter. You will matter. God will matter.

Why Santa is So Real

If you think about it, isn't this why Santa is so real every Christmas morning? Millions of parents just doing their part, serving their own children. And because of this, millions of children are convinced Santa lives. In similar fashion, what if we all decided to do our part in serving three people the way God calls us to in His Word. Would God not become real to them as well?

A Fight to The Finish

And that about wraps it up. God is strong, and he wants you strong. So take everything the Master has set out for you, well-made weapons of the best materials. And put them to use so you will be able to stand up to everything the devil throws your way. This is no afternoon athletic contest that we'll walk away from and forget about in a couple of hours. This is for keeps, a life-or-death fight to the finish against the devil and all his angels. Be prepared. You're up against far more than you can handle on your own. Take all the help you can get, every weapon God has issued, so that when it's all over but shouting you'll still be on your feet. Truth, righteousness, peace, faith, and salvation are more than words. Learn how to apply them. You'll need them throughout your life. God's word is an indispensable weapon. In the same way, prayer is essential in this ongoing warfare. Pray hard and long. Pray for your brothers and sisters. Keep your eyes open. Keep each other's spirits up so that no one falls behind or drops out.

(Ephesians 6:10-18, *MSG*)

Want a sticker?

Inside your being, you know God has called you to champion His cause. When you read of this Generation to Come in Psalm 78, you know without a doubt, you are the fulfillment of this prophecy written thousands of years ago. Now, it is time to wear it and declare it! I have created a sticker that goes on the back window of your car or laptop so everyone in the world will know who you are and what you stand for. It will also help you identify with others who have been called as well. Go to www.theG2C.com/stickers and click on the "Free Sticker" button. We will send it to you in the snail mail and consider you in the fight. In the book of Joshua, just before he was to move Israel across the Jordan and into the promised land, God spoke to him. This is what he said, "Have I not commanded you? Be strong and courageous! Do not tremble or be dismayed, for the Lord your God is with you wherever you go." (Joshua 1:9) It is now time to take the land God has promised you.

The
G2C
TheG2C.com

ACKNOWLEGEMENTS

To Gene Roy, Jeff Clabaugh and the youth group of Pine Valley Community Church. Thank you for your willingness to pilot this book.

To Aaron Keil. Thanks for getting tired of me talking to you about this stuff and telling me to write a book instead. Without your inspiration, I don't think this book would have happened.

To Josh Rose, my sister and dad. Thank you for your honesty about my original title. You were right, teens would be turned off by it and not compelled to read it. It is true, people do judge a book by its cover.

To Stephen Roy for being emphatic about including references to my claims and for challenging me to prove Satan's attack on the United States is real.

To my lovely wife Tanya who read for days looking for any errors in this book. I thank you from the bottom of my heart and am so glad to have you as my soul mate.

To my mentor Stan Nolte. Thank you so much for coming along side of me and helping me design a ministry that values mentoring our youth.

To the men of Outback. I can't begin to express my gratitude for your Godly presence in my life. Thank you so much for your prayers and support.

To Jean-Marie Jobs and The Gap Youth Training. You taught me so much about God and life. I can honestly say before I knew you I was a boy. Twenty years later, I can now look back and say, because of your influence and The Gap, I became a man.

Finally, to my mom. Thanks for being my biggest fan. And, thank you for showing me what it means to have unwavering faith.